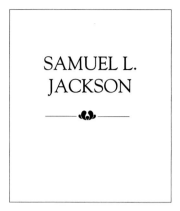

SAMUEL L. JACKSON

SAMUEL L. JACKSON

❦

Tracey E. Dils

CHELSEA HOUSE PUBLISHERS
Philadelphia

To Clarke Wilhelm
who taught me to love the art of film.

Special thanks to Russell Herrold IV
for his assistance in preparing this manuscript.

Chelsea House Publishers

Editor in Chief	Stephen Reginald
Production Manager	Pamela Loos
Art Director	Sara Davis
Director of Photography	Judy L. Hasday
Managing Editor	James D. Gallagher
Senior Production Editor	LeeAnne Gelletly

Staff for SAMUEL L. JACKSON

Senior Editor	Therese De Angelis
Associate Art Director	Takeshi Takahashi
Picture Researcher	Patricia Burns
Cover Illustrator/Designer	Keith Trego

Cover Photo: © Corbis/Jim Bridges

The Chelsea House World Wide Web address is
http://www.chelseahouse.com

First Printing

1 3 5 7 9 8 6 4 2

Dils, Tracey E.
  Samuel L. Jackson / by Tracey E. Dils.
    pp.   cm. — (Black Americans of achievement)
Filmography: p.
Includes bibliographical references and index.
Summary: A biography of the critically acclaimed actor, known for his
work in such films as "Jungle Fever," "Pulp Fiction," and "Star Wars:
Episode I—The Phantom Menace."
ISBN 0-7910-5281-8
      0-7910-5282-6 (pbk.)
1. Jackson, Samuel L.—Juvenile literature. 2. Motion picture actors and
actresses—United States—Biography—Juvenile literature. 3. Afro-
American motion picture actors and actresses—United States—Biogra-
phy—Juvenile literature. [1. Jackson, Samuel L. 2. Actors and actresses.
3. Afro-Americans—Biography.] I. Title. II. Series.
PN2287.J285D55   1999
791.43'028'092—dc21   99-37423
[B]   CIP

CONTENTS

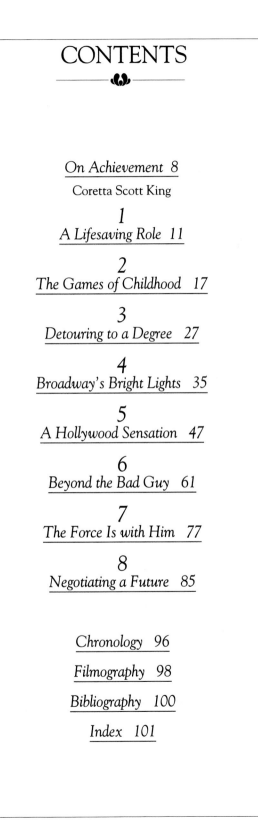

BLACK AMERICANS OF ACHIEVEMENT

HENRY AARON
baseball great

KAREEM ABDUL-JABBAR
basketball great

MUHAMMAD ALI
heavyweight champion

RICHARD ALLEN
religious leader and social activist

MAYA ANGELOU
author

LOUIS ARMSTRONG
musician

ARTHUR ASHE
tennis great

JOSEPHINE BAKER
entertainer

JAMES BALDWIN
author

TYRA BANKS
model

BENJAMIN BANNEKER
scientist and mathematician

COUNT BASIE
bandleader and composer

ANGELA BASSETT
actress

ROMARE BEARDEN
artist

HALLE BERRY
actress

MARY MCLEOD BETHUNE
educator

GEORGE WASHINGTON
CARVER
botanist

JOHNNIE COCHRAN
lawyer

SEAN "PUFFY" COMBS
music producer

BILL COSBY
entertainer

MILES DAVIS
musician

FREDERICK DOUGLASS
abolitionist editor

CHARLES DREW
physician

W. E. B. DU BOIS
scholar and activist

PAUL LAURENCE DUNBAR
poet

DUKE ELLINGTON
bandleader and composer

RALPH ELLISON
author

JULIUS ERVING
basketball great

LOUIS FARRAKHAN
political activist

ELLA FITZGERALD
singer

ARETHA FRANKLIN
entertainer

MORGAN FREEMAN
actor

MARCUS GARVEY
black nationalist leader

JOSH GIBSON
baseball great

WHOOPI GOLDBERG
entertainer

CUBA GOODING JR.
actor

ALEX HALEY
author

PRINCE HALL
social reformer

JIMI HENDRIX
musician

MATTHEW HENSON
explorer

GREGORY HINES
performer

BILLIE HOLIDAY
singer

LENA HORNE
entertainer

WHITNEY HOUSTON
singer and actress

LANGSTON HUGHES
poet

JANET JACKSON
musician

JESSE JACKSON
civil-rights leader and politician

MICHAEL JACKSON
entertainer

SAMUEL L. JACKSON *actor*	JOE LOUIS *heavyweight champion*	ROSA PARKS *civil-rights leader*	TINA TURNER *entertainer*
T. D. JAKES *religious leader*	RONALD MCNAIR *astronaut*	COLIN POWELL *military leader*	ALICE WALKER *author*
JACK JOHNSON *heavyweight champion*	MALCOLM X *militant black leader*	PAUL ROBESON *singer and actor*	MADAM C. J. WALKER *entrepreneur*
MAGIC JOHNSON *basketball great*	BOB MARLEY *musician*	JACKIE ROBINSON *baseball great*	BOOKER T. WASHINGTON *educator*
SCOTT JOPLIN *composer*	THURGOOD MARSHALL *Supreme Court justice*	CHRIS ROCK *comedian and actor*	DENZEL WASHINGTON *actor*
BARBARA JORDAN *politician*	TERRY MCMILLAN *author*	DIANA ROSS *entertainer*	J. C. WATTS *politician*
MICHAEL JORDAN *basketball great*	TONI MORRISON *author*	WILL SMITH *actor*	VANESSA WILLIAMS *singer and actress*
CORETTA SCOTT KING *civil-rights leader*	ELIJAH MUHAMMAD *religious leader*	WESLEY SNIPES *actor*	OPRAH WINFREY *entertainer*
MARTIN LUTHER KING, JR. *civil-rights leader*	EDDIE MURPHY *entertainer*	CLARENCE THOMAS *Supreme Court justice*	TIGER WOODS *golf star*
LEWIS LATIMER *scientist*	JESSE OWENS *champion athlete*	SOJOURNER TRUTH *antislavery activist*	RICHARD WRIGHT *author*
SPIKE LEE *filmmaker*	SATCHEL PAIGE *baseball great*	HARRIET TUBMAN *antislavery activist*	
CARL LEWIS *champion athlete*	CHARLIE PARKER *musician*	NAT TURNER *slave revolt leader*	

ON ACHIEVEMENT

❧

Coretta Scott King

Before you begin this book, I hope you will ask yourself what the word *excellence* means to you. I think it's a question we should all ask, and keep asking as we grow older and change. Because the truest answer to it should never change. When you think of excellence, perhaps you think of success at work; or of becoming wealthy; or meeting the right person, getting married, and having a good family life.

Those goals are worth striving for, but there is a better way to look at excellence. As Martin Luther King Jr. said in one of his last sermons, "I want you to be first in love. I want you to be first in moral excellence. I want you to be first in generosity. If you want to be important, wonderful. If you want to be great, wonderful. But recognize that he who is greatest among you shall be your servant."

My husband knew that the true meaning of achievement is service. When I met him, in 1952, he was already ordained as a Baptist minister and was working toward a doctoral degree at Boston University. I was studying at the New England Conservatory and dreamed of accomplishments in music. We married a year later, and after I graduated the following year we moved to Montgomery, Alabama. We didn't know it then, but our notions of achievement were about to undergo a dramatic change.

You may have read or heard about what happened next. What began with the boycott of a local bus line grew into a national crusade, and by the time he was assassinated in 1968 my husband had fashioned a black movement powerful enough to shatter forever the practice of racial segregation. What you may not have read about is where he learned to resist injustice without compromising his religious beliefs.

He adopted a strategy of nonviolence from a man of a different race, who lived in a different country and even practiced a different religion. The man was Mahatma Gandhi, the great leader of India, who devoted his life to serving humanity in the spirit of love and nonviolence. It was in these principles that Martin discovered his method for social reform. More than anything else, those two principles were the key to his achievements.

These books are about African Americans who served society through the excellence of their achievements. They form part of the rich history of black men and women in America—a history of stunning accomplishments in every field of human endeavor, from literature and art to science, industry, education, diplomacy, athletics, jurisprudence, even polar exploration.

Not all of the people in this history had the same ideals, but I think you will find that all of them had something in common. Like Martin Luther King Jr., they all decided to become "drum majors" and serve humanity. In that principle—whether it was expressed in books, inventions, or song—they found a goal and a guide outside themselves that showed them a way to serve others instead of living only for themselves.

Reading the stories of these courageous men and women not only helps us discover the principles that we will use to guide our own lives; it also teaches us about our black heritage and about America itself. It is crucial for us to know the heroes and heroines of our history and to realize that the price we paid in our struggle for equality in America was dear. But we must also understand that we have gotten as far as we have partly because America's democratic system and ideals made it possible.

We are still struggling with racism and prejudice. But the great men and women in this series are a tribute to the spirit of the country in which they have flourished. And that makes their stories special and worth knowing.

1

A LIFESAVING ROLE

"**M**AMA! GIMME SOME MONEY," the black actor shouts from the big screen of the movie theater. "I ain't goin' nowhere until you gimme some money." His bloodshot eyes are round with rage. His hands are quivering as he throws open cabinet after cabinet, empties drawer after drawer, in a desperate search for cash. All his mother can do is stand by in terror.

The next time he begs and pleads with his mother to give him money, he does so in a most unusual way—he asks her to dance. And in this strange and intimate moment, both she and the audience watching the movie begin to melt. Although the character is a hopeless crack addict, there is a humanity about him that is as touching as it is repelling.

The actor behind the addict is Samuel L. Jackson, who plays Gator Purify, a minor character in Spike Lee's film *Jungle Fever*. The movie tells the story of a married black architect named Flipper (played by Wesley Snipes) and his affair with a white secretary (played by Annabella Sciorra). But it is Jackson's performance as Snipes's crack-addicted brother that captured most of the critical and popular attention the movie received.

In Jackson's Gator, audience members get a terrifying glimpse into the life of a crack addict, a life many cannot even imagine. At the same time, there is something eerily sympathetic and familiar about

One of Jackson's greatest achievements was overcoming his addiction to alcohol and other drugs after completing a rehabilitation program in 1990. "Sam is a walking miracle," a friend says about Jackson's recovery.

the derelict Gator's desperation and the way he manipulates his family—always promising to pay back the money he owes them—that draws the audience in. Gator's bold-faced admission that he is going to get high no matter what lends a horrifying matter-of-factness to the character.

Most amazing, perhaps, is how realistic and human Gator seems. His rail-thin body, his shaky hands, and the look of shame on his face when his brother finds him getting high in a crackhouse allow the audience to see not only a crack addict but also the human being deep inside.

The critics raved about Samuel L. Jackson's performance in *Jungle Fever*. "Samuel Jackson's blood-curdling performance is the best in a film of superb performances," wrote Jack Kroll of *Newsweek*. "With his eyes like bombed-out moons, and the spooky, sardonic little dance he does to worm money from his mother or brother, Gator is a demon of desperation."

Jackson's performance also caught the attention of the Cannes Film Festival Committee. Cannes, France, hosts the most respected international film festival in the world, and its annual awards ceremony is equal in importance and prestige to the Academy Awards.

Jackson didn't expect to win anything at Cannes. He had already been passed over for an Academy Award, which did not surprise him since *Jungle Fever* was a small, independent film made by producer Spike Lee, a critically acclaimed filmmaker but not a Hollywood insider. In fact, the Cannes Film Festival did not even have an award category for supporting actor, the kind of role Jackson had played in *Jungle Fever*. As Jackson told *Premiere* magazine in 1995:

> The night before Spike left for the Cannes festival, he kept insisting, "You're gonna win something!" And I said, "Spike, they don't give supporting-actor awards at the Cannes Film Festival." For the next few days, I kept roaming around New York like I always did: doing auditions. One afternoon, I phoned my agent to see if I

had any callbacks. "I think people from the Associated Press are looking for you," she said. . . . "They created an award for you [at Cannes]."

As the crack-addicted Gator in Spike Lee's 1991 film Jungle Fever, *Jackson tries to convince his mother, Lucinda (played by Ruby Dee), to loan him money.*

Samuel Jackson's Gator had impressed the Cannes panel of judges so much that they created a supporting actor commendation just for him. The role—and the award—would catapult him to stardom and turn him into a Hollywood phenomenon. The Cannes award wasn't the only accolade he received for playing Gator: the New York Film Critics Circle followed suit that year by honoring Jackson with another Best Supporting Actor award.

What the public and the critics didn't know, however, was just how much Jackson had relied on his own experience to create the character of Gator Purify. "I knew who [Gator] was," Jackson told

Premiere. "In a very literal sense. The easy part was doing the drug part of the role."

And why was it so easy? Because Samuel L. Jackson, like Gator, had faced his own drug demons. In fact, the part of Gator was the first film role that Jackson had played "straight"; that is, without being under the influence of alcohol or other drugs. As a struggling actor and a new husband and father, Jackson says, he let the stress and competition of show business get to him, and he turned to taking drugs and engaging in other forms of destructive behavior. "I was staying out. Not coming home, . . . drinking, drugging, womanizing, doing all these things to make myself feel good about myself except the one thing that I should have been doing: I should have been putting myself in a healthier acting situation by getting my *own* job."

What made matters worse for Jackson was that alcohol and other drugs seemed to be a routine part of being an actor. Drinking alcohol at lunch, smoking pot on breaks, and doing coke before and after shows was so common among those in the business that Jackson didn't even consider himself an addict. After all, he told himself, he wasn't robbing his kid's piggy bank or committing crimes to support his habit. That's what junkies did, he thought. Instead, he was working hard and functioning fairly well.

After Jackson started smoking crack, however, his drug use became desperate—and life-threatening. One day, his wife, LaTanya, found him passed out in the kitchen while cocaine cooked on the stove. She quickly called for help and got Samuel into a drug rehabilitation program.

Being in "rehab" got Jackson off alcohol and other drugs, but playing Gator helped him come to terms with his former, out-of-control behavior. "Doing all of the research I did for Gator—going to crack houses, checking out what was going on around my house on 143rd Street in Harlem and really getting to know people who were caught in that trap—was a wake-up call for me," Jackson said in 1993. "Gator was close to me, and playing him was kind of cathartic. The experience got me clean." Jackson's friend Leonard Thomas agrees. "Sam is a walking miracle right now," Thomas has said. "He should have been dead [from drug abuse]."

The role of Gator Purify not only brought Samuel L. Jackson well-deserved critical success and landed his name on the lists of Hollywood's top producers. In many ways it also saved his life by giving him the courage and the motivation to stay off drugs, so that he could reach his full potential as an actor and human being.

It's no wonder Jackson's portrayal of Gator is so compelling.

2

THE GAMES OF CHILDHOOD

SAMUEL LEROY JACKSON was born on December 21, 1948, in Washington, D.C., the son of Elizabeth Jackson and a young enlisted army man. The couple separated when Samuel was still very young. According to Jackson, his father "was never there. His story was that he had been in the Army and my mom tried to get money from him for me and he got out of the Army rather than pay. He blamed her for his career being ruined because she wanted money for me." Jackson's father later settled in Kansas City, Kansas. Samuel saw him only once more in his life, after his own daughter was born.

Without child-support payments, Elizabeth Jackson found it next to impossible to raise young Samuel on her salary as a domestic, so she sent him to live in Chattanooga, Tennessee, with his maternal grandparents. A sleepy railroad town in the early 1800s, Chattanooga experienced a population boom after the Civil War. The town had been the site of a pivotal military campaign known as the Battle of Chickamauga and Chattanooga, during which the Union had gained most of eastern Tennessee. Many Union soldiers, black and white, remained in the town after the war ended. By the 1950s, when Samuel arrived in Chattanooga, it had become a major industrial center with a well-established black community, complete with its own social hierarchy.

When Samuel was three years old, his mother sent him to the factory town of Chattanooga, Tennessee, to live with his maternal grandparents. The strict segregation of blacks from whites was so ingrained in the townspeople of Chattanooga that Jackson remembers it not as traumatic but as a "way of life."

Chuck Connors (left) in the title role of the TV series The Rifleman, *with Charlton Heston (right). Samuel L. Jackson's passion for acting developed in part from his love of TV westerns like* The Rifleman *and* Wanted— Dead or Alive.

Samuel lived with his grandparents on Lookout Street in an older neighborhood of two-story homes that had been built in the 1880s near downtown Chattanooga. The neighborhood was the kind where people took responsibility not only for their own families but also for those of their neighbors. "The whole neighborhood was in charge of all the kids," Jackson says of his childhood community. "[The person whose] house you were in front of had the right to discipline you, to love you, whatever."

Chattanooga was also steeped in musical tradition. It was said that the great blues singer Bessie Smith, who was born there in 1894, sang for money on the corner of Market Street before her career took off. The great opera singer Roland Hayes, the first African-American concert artist to receive international recognition, also hailed from Chattanooga, and he returned frequently to perform there during the 1950s. Decades later, the rap singer Usher also hailed from Chattanooga.

Like almost all southern towns during the 1950s, however, Chattanooga was strictly segregated. Blacks were relegated to separate restrooms, drinking fountains, and restaurants. Of all the city's parks, blacks were allowed in only one: Lincoln Park. And though black settlers had established the first school in Chattanooga—Howard School—white children did not attend there, and it was considered inferior to the white schools in the area.

Such segregation was more than a matter of tradition; it was officially enforced by a legal code known as Jim Crow laws (named after an insultingly ignorant black character in a popular minstrel show of the 19th century). Unofficially, segregation was enforced by the terrible threat of lynchings or beatings. Blacks could rarely maintain friendships or any other kind of equal relationship with whites. Indeed, having such relationships could be dangerous, even deadly.

Samuel found out very early how dangerous it could be for a black person in Chattanooga to have contact with whites:

> When I was four or five, I whistled at a white girl from our porch. My grandmother, my mom, my aunt, everybody was out of the house, snatching me up, hitting me. Because I could have been killed for that. There were lots of things that I could not do. Places I could not go.

After that, Samuel told *People* magazine in 1996, "the only white people I came into contact with were store owners. White kids would ride the bus by us on the way to their school and throw whatever they had at us. We'd throw whatever we had at them. We didn't think of it as trauma. That was a way of life."

Like many large southern towns during the 1950s and 1960s, Chattanooga had its share of civil rights demonstrations. Here, a lone black man sits in protest at a "whites-only" lunch counter. Packages of napkins have been placed on the stools to discourage other protesters from joining him.

Although Elizabeth Jackson didn't join her son in Chattanooga until he was 10 years old, she still exerted a strong influence on his life. "I didn't dress hip like the other kids. My mom had standards to meet and I was more afraid of her than I was of other kids," the actor recalls. In fact, Jackson claims, he wore whatever Elizabeth wanted him to wear: knickers, argyle kneesocks, and turtlenecks. He admits that he was a bit of a nerd. "My mother never allowed me to buy my own clothes or even choose them. My job was to go to school. I didn't get into trouble because I didn't want to cause my family embarrassment or grief."

Even so, Samuel managed to have his share of good times and to develop his dramatic side as well. He had begun acting while he was still a boy in Chattanooga, but he didn't like it right away. He had a bad stuttering problem that made him the butt of many of his classmates' jokes. The teasing made Samuel feel so uncomfortable that for an entire year he didn't talk at all. He was in fourth grade when he finally received speech therapy, which helped him overcome his stutter. It wasn't long after that he began to display his talent for acting, appearing as Humpty Dumpty and the Sugar Plum Fairy in plays that his aunt, Edna Eldridge, produced at James A. Henry Elementary School. The only classes he didn't enjoy, Elizabeth Jackson recalls, were his aunt's modern dance classes. "Something about that modern dance he didn't take to much," she laughs.

Even when Samuel was involved in neighborhood games with other kids, he was acting. One of Jackson's favorite pastimes was imitating the main characters he saw on TV westerns such as *The Rifleman* and *Wanted—Dead or Alive*. "I had a *Rifleman* gun, so . . . I was [actor] Chuck Connors," Jackson said. "I had a *Wanted—Dead or Alive* gun, and so I was [actor] Steve McQueen for a while. I could be anybody I wanted to be."

One time, Jackson remembers, he played at this game a little too earnestly. In an attempt at realism, Jackson smeared some ketchup on a cotton pad and wore the pad on his head during a game of war. The women along Lookout Street who were keeping an eye on Samuel and his friends thought the boy had been badly injured. When they discovered the truth, Samuel got in deep trouble. But it was during those years of acting out television scenes that Jackson perfected a dramatic technique he has become known for—dying. "I died a lot when I was a kid," he says. "I

Samuel was a popular student and an accomplished athlete at Riverside High School, shown here in an early photo. Though friends and teachers predicted that Samuel would one day make a name for himself, no one imagined that he would become an acclaimed actor.

played those games. We'd fall off things and die. We'd try and find a hill you could roll down and die. We'd stagger, stagger, fall against stuff, stagger, do that whole thing."

Jackson completed his studies at James A. Henry Elementary School under the guidance of teacher Mabel Scruggs, who was also the boy's Sunday-school teacher at Wiley Memorial United Methodist Church. Mrs. Scruggs remembers Samuel as "a very good student, very bright and . . . always inquisitive." His good manners and conscientious nature also earned him the respect of his fellow students.

In spite of his polite ways, Samuel was no pushover. He was the kind of child who stood up for his rights. Once, when he received a poor grade that he didn't think was fair, he refused to accept the teacher's assessment. Instead, he reasoned with her until she became convinced that he really deserved a higher grade.

Samuel discovered the movies when he was in junior high school. Elizabeth, who had gotten a job in Chattanooga as a clothing buyer for a children's store, loved going to the movie theater, and she often took her son with her—but only to the all-black theaters, such as the Grand and the Liberty. Today Jackson recalls that some of the films featuring blacks and whites interacting were edited or changed for black audiences. One film, *Band of Angels* (1957), starring the respected black actor Sidney Poitier and white actress Yvonne DeCarlo, originally included a scene in which Poitier's character slaps DeCarlo's character during a heated argument. "He's become a Union soldier and comes back [from the fighting] and she's sitting there pretending to be the white mistress of the house, and he slaps her," Jackson relates. "Now, that was a big thing in the South. We heard about this scene!" But in the version shown in Chattanooga and elsewhere in the South, the portion in which Poitier hits DeCarlo was cut.

During Jackson's high school years, a wave of civil rights protests was sweeping southern cities. Inspired by Martin Luther King Jr., who advocated organized nonviolent protest against racial segregation and discrimination, blacks throughout America—and especially in the South—were conducting "sit-ins" at lunch counters in whites-only restaurants, organizing boycotts of segregated buses, arranging freedom rallies, and planning protest marches. The goal of these actions was to end legal segregation, so that blacks would have equal opportunities in employment, education, sports, politics, and other arenas.

Although most of the civil rights activity in Tennessee was centered to the north of Chattanooga in Nashville, the town did witness its share of demonstrations. As early as 1905, before the mass civil rights movement of the 1950s and 1960s had developed, blacks in Chattanooga had staged a streetcar boycott. And in the early 1960s, local blacks held a sit-in at a Woolworth's lunch counter in downtown Chattanooga. While Samuel Jackson had certainly heard about the movement that was swirling around him, it didn't affect what was a fairly average high school career. "It didn't seem abnormal," Jackson said of the racial problem where he grew up. "You knew who the racists were, you knew the people who would harass you because you were black, and the people who didn't care whether you were black, white, or whatever. It was pretty cut and dried."

Jackson attended Riverside High School, a new, three-year high school that brought together black students from several different areas of Chattanooga. Samuel had hoped to attend Howard High, a school that was far enough away from home for him to take a bus. But when Riverside opened up, Samuel was forced to trudge to school once again through downtown Chattanooga.

As a new school, Riverside High School was faced with the challenge of developing its own traditions, from establishing social clubs and fraternities to inventing its own slogans and cheers, and even forming its own brand-new sports teams. It was as a member of the new track team that Samuel gained popularity among his classmates. The team, which Samuel describes as a "ragtag" group of athletes, faced serious competition from the more established African-American high schools in the area. But Jackson's talent for completing high hurdles helped Riverside win third place in its region and earned him a Christian Athlete of the Year award during his senior year.

Samuel's former classmates have described him as a churchgoer, a likable and down-to-earth person. But none of his friends would have predicted that Jackson would make a name for himself as an actor. Classmate Rheuben Taylor says that he would have predicted that Samuel would pursue a music career instead. "He was an excellent trumpet player and we just assumed that would be what he would pursue," Taylor recalled in an interview with Entertainment Television. Another classmate, Lamarr Partridge, believed that "if he didn't choose music, he would end up in medicine or something. . . . He is a very bright individual."

Even Jackson's mother didn't see an acting career in her son's future. She encouraged him to study medicine, hoping that one day he would become Chattanooga's first black pediatrician. "But that didn't go over too well," she says. When Samuel began preparing to attend college, he chose an entirely different path and enrolled as a marine biology major at Morehouse College in Atlanta, Georgia. Acting was probably the farthest thing from Samuel Jackson's mind as well.

3
DETOURING TO A DEGREE

A FTER A SUMMER spent working as a night-shift enamel mixer for a company that put finishes on stoves in Chattanooga, Samuel must have thought of Morehouse College as an oasis. He couldn't wait to join the pep squad at Morehouse and to begin his coursework in marine biology.

Located just a mile west of downtown Atlanta, Morehouse is a large, private, all-male college with a predominantly black enrollment. Often called the "Harvard of the South," Morehouse is the largest black male college in the world. It is well-known not only for its excellent science and engineering programs but also for its role in helping to shape the careers of young African-American men. Martin Luther King Jr. and Spike Lee are among the distinguished graduates of Morehouse.

The college is also known for its tradition of brotherhood, which dates back to its founding in 1867. Like all Morehouse freshman, Samuel most likely participated in the traditional "Spirit Night," a ceremony in which freshmen link arms and form a circle that the upperclassmen try to break. The symbolic ritual encourages Morehouse students to form a sense of kinship and to trust their new classmates as friends.

Despite Morehouse's strong tradition of brotherhood, in late 1969, when Samuel Jackson arrived on

At first, Jackson viewed acting as an enjoyable occupation. After working in the theaters of Atlanta, however, he began pursuing it as a serious career.

campus, the college was being torn apart by student demonstrations over the role of the United States in the Vietnam War. Many Americans, especially college students, saw the war as unjustifiable. Moreover, some of the country's black leaders were claiming that America's activities in Vietnam mirrored the oppression that had been inflicted upon blacks in the American South.

It further angered many African Americans that blacks were going to war in disproportionate numbers compared to whites, and that blacks were sustaining the greatest number of casualties. African Americans made up just 10 percent of the country's population, yet they made up about 20 percent of the U.S. forces in Vietnam. Most of them had been drafted, and even some who failed the military's selective service exam were still admitted into the army, especially in southern states. The blacks who saw combat in Vietnam were often in more dangerous situations than most white soldiers, and they were therefore more likely to be wounded or killed.

The assassination of Martin Luther King on April 4, 1968, combined with the outrage over the atrocities of the Vietnam War, galvanized many Americans into taking action over racial inequality. Among the more militant black groups was the Black Power movement, which aimed to fight back, physically if necessary, against racist policies.

In Atlanta, Samuel L. Jackson, who had come to Morehouse to study marine biology, instead found himself at the heart of the racial protest movement. "The Vietnam War was escalating, as were the love movement, peace movement, and black-militant movement," Samuel told an interviewer for *Cosmopolitan* magazine in 1994. "My roommate and I were throwing Molotov cocktails [a dangerous homemade explosive]; he was arrested and sent to jail." Jackson escaped punishment—that time. But at the end of his sophomore year, he tried a protest

approach that was even more radical: he and 30 other Morehouse students took the college's board of trustees hostage.

The students had important grievances, Jackson says. They wanted a black studies program at the college and student representation on the board of trustees. When the administrators refused to talk to them, the students took over the building. As Jackson tells it, "We went into the building where they were meeting, padlocked the doors from the inside, and told them that they weren't leaving until we talked to them."

Among the trustees were Martin Luther King Sr. and several federal judges. Although the National Guard was called in to force the students out of the

While attending Morehouse College, Samuel became caught up in the atmosphere of confrontation that swept across America over racial discrimination and the country's involvement in the Vietnam War. In this 1969 photo, a young protester is arrested by Georgia state police in Atlanta after his involvement in a civil rights demonstration.

Samuel describes meeting his wife, LaTanya Richardson, as "love at first sight." The two met while participating in a joint theater production between Morehouse and Spelman Colleges, and they soon became inseparable.

building, the Guardsmen never came in. According to Jackson, he and his fellow students weren't dangerous and did not intend to harm anyone. "We didn't have guns or anything," he said in an Entertainment Television interview.

After two days, the student protesters released the trustees. Jackson was suspended for his participation in the takeover. But when his suspension period was over, he went directly back to Morehouse. He missed college life, and he also knew that if he stayed out of school too long, he would risk being drafted and end up in Vietnam.

After Samuel returned to Morehouse, he changed his major from marine biology to acting. It was a strange choice for him. Aside from the parts he had in his aunt's elementary school plays, Samuel had appeared in only one production: a Morehouse version of Bertolt Brecht's *Threepenny Opera*. He had auditioned for a part in the play not because he loved the theater, but because a professor of public speaking offered him extra credit to perform in it. In addition, no one had ever suggested, let alone encouraged, Samuel to try acting, and that may have been part of its appeal. "No one had ever told me I could be an actor. . . . It wasn't a viable career for a young black person," he recalls.

Jackson pursued his newly discovered calling ardently, despite his mother's appeals to study in a field that could provide a "real" job for him some day. "I would not major in something else so I could change careers when things got a little rough," Jackson told the *Chattanooga Free Press* in 1995. "I had to do what I did. I had other skills I could do to keep me [going;] I built sets, hung lights, helped people with costumes. I never took a job waiting tables."

Before long, Jackson had immersed himself in the theater life of Atlanta. At first it was a fun, almost make-believe world for him. But when he realized that acting could be a legitimate career for him, he changed his outlook. "When I started to do street theater, and then I started doing children's theater and repertory theater at this other company, I realized that I could make a living doing it, and I could have a great time. That made me kind of serious about it," he explains.

Samuel took advantage of every theater opportunity he could find. "Everything else became insignificant," he said in 1998. "I threw myself into it. When I got up in the morning, I was at the theater in the drama department and I was building sets all day, and I would go and do this other job at the children's theater and then I had to come back to the theater at the school, and after that we had our own guerrilla street theater that we used to rehearse until 3 in the morning. . . . It totally became part of my fabric, being an actor."

It was during this hectic period that he met LaTanya Richardson. LaTanya attended Spelman College, Morehouse's sister school, and the two schools often cooperated in theater productions. LaTanya had known of Samuel from his days as a member of the school pep squad, and when she first noticed him onstage during an audition, she wondered, "What's cheerleader boy doing on my stage?" And though she wasn't greatly impressed by his performance, she was struck by his good looks. "He was very, very fine," LaTanya said in 1998. "[He] had this huge Afro, little bitty round sunglasses and long sideburns." She compared his looks to those of Linc Hayes, a black character on a popular TV drama of the late 1960s and early 1970s called *The Mod Squad.* "He was tall, which was great, tall and lithe," LaTanya remembers fondly.

According to a 1997 *New York Times* interview with Jackson, the meeting was almost "love at first sight." Although LaTanya didn't think highly of Samuel's acting abilities—in 1971 she and a group of her friends once heckled him during a performance at the Black Image Theater—Samuel and LaTanya became inseparable from that moment on. After Samuel graduated from Morehouse in 1972, the couple combined their talents and their political views to form their own community theater company, which they called the Just Us Theater. There they produced and performed in plays that carried black activist messages.

Samuel also managed to wrangle a small part for himself in a movie called *Together for Days,* starring Clifton Davis and Lois Chiles. And folks in Chattanooga were surprised to see their childhood friend in a commercial for a southern fast-food chain called Krystal Hamburgers. According to the commercial, Krystal Hamburgers were different, and Jackson's single line, "It's these little cooked onions," was meant to be a testament to the hamburger's distinctive flavor.

As successful as he had been in Atlanta, however, Samuel Jackson didn't intend to stay there. Before long, he began setting his course for a far different city. His goal was to test his acting talent on the stages of New York City.

4

BROADWAY'S BRIGHT LIGHTS

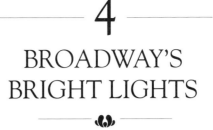

SAMUEL JACKSON AND LaTanya Richardson moved to New York City on Halloween night in 1976. They settled in Harlem, and although Samuel spent a month or so working as a security guard in a Manhattan office building to make ends meet, the two actors broke into New York theater in an amazingly short time. Only a few months after arriving in New York, they both found acting work, and before long, they were performing regularly with the Negro Ensemble Company and the New York Shakespeare Festival.

The "real world" of acting in New York was far different from what Samuel had experienced at Morehouse, and he reveled in the wealth of opportunities available to him. He told the *Chattanooga Free Press* in 1995:

> When I got out in the real world, you rehearsed six days a week, eight hours a day, and there are so many things you can discover about a character while you are working on a daily basis. We were just learning the lines and going out there and saying them [in college]. Then [when] you get out in the theater world, you are challenged—[you need to learn] where this character is coming from, where he is going, what kind of attitudes he has, what kind of experiences he's had.
>
> Consequently, the audience sees all the person, not just a shell giving the right facial expressions and right vocal inflections and I kind of carry that with me to my characters now, because we don't have the time

Samuel L. Jackson (left) menaces Spike Lee in a scene from Lee's film Mo' Better Blues.

to rehearse like we did in the theater. I make up biographies for my characters the same way I did then.

Jackson's formula for making his characters seem more vivid must have worked. He earned good reviews for nearly every play in which he appeared, including off-Broadway dramas such as *The Mighty Gents*, Richard Wesley's play about a group of derelicts in a New Jersey ghetto; a version of Bertolt Brecht's *Mother Courage* adapted by black playwright Ntozake Shange; and two productions of the Negro Ensemble Company, *District Line* and *Home*.

In 1980, Samuel L. Jackson and LaTanya Richardson were married in a New York ceremony, with more than one thousand friends, relatives, and fellow actors looking on. Soon after, Samuel received what seemed like a big break: a role in the film *Ragtime*, which starred the legendary actor James Cagney. Jackson landed a part as a gang member. He flew to London to film the movie and was put up in a nice flat (apartment) for several months. Although the role was minor, Jackson began to believe that his film career was finally taking off.

But it was his stage role in Charles Fuller's *A Soldier's Play* that transformed Samuel's early career. On that set he met Morgan Freeman, who became a lifelong friend and a role model for acting. The first time Samuel saw Freeman onstage, he recalled in 1998, he knew that Freeman's acting style was "the exact way that I need to learn to act so that I can affect a person the way he is affecting me." Freeman became more than a role model for Samuel; he was also a kind of mentor. Morgan Freeman was the first person to convince Samuel that he could succeed as an actor.

While performing in *A Soldier's Play*, Samuel met another man who would play a critical part in the actor's success as a film star. After a performance one night, Spike Lee, who was at the time a film student at New York University, came backstage and raved

about how great Samuel's performance had been. Spike told Samuel that he had big plans: he was going to create movies that would turn the filmmaking world upside down. When he got to that point, Spike insisted, he wanted Jackson in his films. After all, he claimed, Morehouse graduates should stick together.

In the meantime, Samuel took bit parts in a number of films and television programs, including a minor role on a short-lived TV show called *Movin' On* and the character of a villain in several episodes of *Spenser for Hire*. For a time, Samuel was even Bill Cosby's rehearsal stand-in on the wildly popular *Cosby Show*. The position paid well and allowed him to pursue his theater work when he wasn't required on the *Cosby* set.

In 1982, Samuel and LaTanya's child, Zoe Jackson, was born. Overjoyed by the birth of his daughter and mindful of his own father's absence while he was growing up, Samuel was determined to be the best

Samuel L. Jackson (far left) as a member of a criminal gang in the 1981 movie Ragtime. *The movie was based on author E. L. Doctorow's 1975 novel about turn-of-the-century America.*

Jackson's "big break" came with his 1981 stage performance in Charles Fuller's A Soldier's Play. *He is shown here, third from right, next to another up-and-coming star, Denzel Washington (on Jackson's immediate right).*

father he could be. "My father abandoned us when I was just a child," he remembered in 1997. "I promised myself when we had Zoe that I'd be there for her no matter what."

Although he was delighted with his new role as father, Jackson was growing increasingly unhappy with the course that his professional life was taking. For years after his work in *Ragtime*, he received only bit parts and offers for cameo appearances (brief film appearances that are limited to a single scene). He appeared in two Eddie Murphy productions, the concert film *Raw* (1987) and the movie *Coming to America* (1988), and played villainous characters in *A Shock to the System* (1990), *Def by Temptation* (1990), *The Exorcist III* (1990), and *The Return of Superfly* (1990). In the movie *Sea of Love* (1989), starring Al Pacino, he impressed both Pacino and the film's directors with his improvisational abilities. Yet when the film was edited, Jackson's role was reduced to one very brief scene, and in the credits he was listed simply as "Black Guy." Jackson also began to grow concerned about being typecast as a "bad guy," but LaTanya offered sound advice that her husband took to heart. "She made me see that Humphrey Bogart and James Cagney made whole careers of being villains," he told an interviewer for *People* magazine in 1991.

The small parts and low-budget films in which Jackson was appearing were unsatisfying for the energetic actor, so in 1987, when an opportunity arose for him to return briefly to stage acting, he took it. Playwright August Wilson tapped him for his play *The Piano Lesson*, in which Jackson's character, Boy Willie, attempts to sell his family's heirloom piano that is kept in his sister's haunted house. Jackson agreed to sign on as a cast member with the Yale Repertory Theater's version of the play in New Haven, Connecticut. It was understood that when Wilson's play went to Broadway, actor Charles Dutton would replace Jackson as Boy Willie. Dutton had already been contracted to perform in *The Piano Lesson* after he completed shooting for the film *Alien*.

Nevertheless, Samuel L. Jackson felt a huge blow when he stepped aside to become an understudy to Dutton during the Broadway run of the play. Watching Dutton receive applause and ovations each night from the audience "made me crazy," recalled Jackson in 1995. "I sat backstage, feeling sorry for myself." And when Dutton was nominated for a prestigious Tony Award, Jackson's feelings of disappointment and competitiveness overwhelmed him. Some years earlier, Jackson had begun using alcohol, marijuana, and cocaine in a vain effort to escape from his career frustrations, but now his depression pushed him further into a downward spiral. He started using more of the drugs, and more frequently.

Samuel L. Jackson in the Yale Repertory Theater's 1987 production of The Piano Lesson. *Although Jackson knew that he would be replaced by another actor when the play moved to Broadway, he was disheartened nonetheless to watch actor Charles Dutton take over the role.*

For a while Jackson had managed to hide his drug use. According to his friend Leonard Thomas, during this period Jackson "was a functioning drug addict. He could get high and go onstage and do his job and get high some more." Among the minor roles that Samuel took at this time was one that would eventually give him the film break he'd been hoping for. Spike Lee, whom Jackson had met years earlier while performing in *A Soldier's Play*, had begun producing his own independent films. Though Jackson had been overlooked for roles in Lee's early productions, such as the breakthrough 1986 film *She's Gotta Have It*, Lee cast him in the 1988 film *School Daze*, a satirical look at an all-black college similar to Morehouse,

Lee and Jackson's alma mater. Jackson's role was a small one—he played a town resident who resented the local college students—but Lee liked Jackson's work enough to cast him in two more films, as Señor Love Daddy in *Do the Right Thing* (1989) and as Madlock in *Mo' Better Blues* (1990), which starred Denzel Washington.

During the filming of *Mo' Better Blues*, Jackson severely injured his knee when his leg became caught between the doors of a New York subway car. While his leg was stuck inside the car and the rest of him was still on the platform outside, the train began moving and pulled Jackson along with it. Passengers in the car attempted to free Jackson, but they were unsuccessful. Eventually someone tugged on an emergency cord to stop the train, but by then it had dragged Samuel 150 feet along the platform. His badly injured knee required surgery, and he had to wear a knee brace for some time. (Several years later, Jackson sued the city's transportation department and was awarded a half-million-dollar settlement for the injury.)

Meanwhile Jackson's drug use continued. Even Charles Dutton, his colleague from *The Piano Lesson*, figured that Samuel would eventually "snap out" of his addiction on his own. "As low as he got at times into that barrel of drug addiction, I knew Sam was going to come out of it, because he seemed to have a sparkle in his eye," Dutton recalled in 1998. But soon Jackson was completely out of control. He lost a lead role in August Wilson's next play, *Two Trains Running*, because, he says, he showed up at too many auditions with bloodshot eyes and smelling of beer. He went to work "blasted out of my mind feeling sorry for myself and it brought me down quicker than anything else could have." Sometimes, he wouldn't even make it home at night; he stayed out drinking, doing drugs, and getting involved with women.

According to his friend Leonard Thomas, Jackson's addictions had "escalated to a point where he couldn't cover it up, where he got exposed. Jackson was faced with an important choice: Were drugs more important than his family? Were they more important than life itself?" Indeed, Jackson's drug addiction and womanizing were devastating to his wife and young daughter. LaTanya, Samuel has since said, refers to that era in their marriage as the "Villa in Hell." He explains that during this time his wife felt that he had "reserved [a place] for her and our daughter" in this terrible world of his own making. "I was mad," Jackson told *Premiere* magazine in 1995. "I was crazed. I was not happy with who I was. As a result, [LaTanya] and [Zoe] paid a lot of taxes for me doing crazed things to myself that transferred to them."

Finally Jackson hit rock bottom. After LaTanya found him passed out in their kitchen, Jackson was sure that he was going to die. But LaTanya called a friend who was a counselor at a rehab clinic and arranged for a bed for her husband. Samuel didn't resist—he was in no shape to argue anyway. He didn't realize how "dead-tired" he had been from his drug abuse and misbehavior until he reached the rehab center. He also realized that "it was time to wake up and do something else." He committed himself to recovery.

Despite his strong desire to reform, Jackson's commitment to recovering from drug abuse didn't come easily. Having spent years under the influence of various drugs, he worried that his personality would change for the worse when he became clean. "When you're in rehab, you worry about little junk," he recalled in a 1998 Entertainment Television interview. "Am I going to be as cool as I used to be? Am I going to be as much fun as I used to be? Will I still be able to dance and enjoy music like I used to?" Jackson soon found that he could not only do all the things he used to do but he could also do them better and enjoy them more. For example, he remembers the first time

With the help of his family and friends—especially his wife, LaTanya—Samuel fully recovered from his drug addictions and dedicated himself to reforming his destructive behavior.

after his recovery when he actually could make out and understand the lyrics to a favorite song.

Samuel L. Jackson was determined to stay clean, in part because he never wanted to go through rehab again. The support of his friends and family helped him reach his goal. "There's been a circle of prayer around his life," his friend Leonard Thomas has said. LaTanya forgave her husband for his drug use and the resulting mistreatment of his family. "I had committed to this relationship and that meant that anything I could do to make sure that this relationship succeeded, no matter what, I was going to do," LaTanya said in a recent interview. With this kind of encouragement, Jackson got clean, devoted himself to his family once more, and, with renewed energy and conviction, threw himself back into acting.

And in 1991, when Spike Lee offered Jackson the part of Gator Purify in *Jungle Fever*, Samuel L. Jackson knew that he was being offered a rare opportunity—the chance to perform while sober and at the same time draw on his experience to create a believable, even sympathetic, character who had an addiction problem. The opportunity was so important that he was initially afraid to take the role. He wasn't certain that he could succeed without using drugs. He wondered whether he even knew how to perform without being under the influence of drugs.

As Gator Purify, Jackson delivered the most impressive performance of his career. Moreover, he created a character that was so true to life that moviegoers saw Gator as a real person. Several people who had seen *Jungle Fever* later approached the actor and told him that they "knew" Gator. "People were constantly telling me that Gator was their brother, their cousin, their son, their husband," Jackson said in 1995.

Jackson was generous in sharing both his acting expertise and the wisdom that he had gained from his addiction experience. *Jungle Fever* was actress Halle Berry's first film, and she had an extremely difficult role: that of Gator's foul-mouthed and promiscuous girlfriend. Jackson stood by her, says Berry. "He was there for me, not only as a person but as an actor. He knew that this was a hard situation for me, a character that I knew nothing about, and he obviously knew a lot about, and he took me under his wing." And when the film was released, it was Jackson's performance as Gator Purify that earned the highest critical acclaim. Morgan Freeman, Jackson's idol, said of the younger man's performance, "Bam—*Jungle Fever*—Whoa. He had arrived."

Jackson later described his screen performance in *Jungle Fever* as the first one in which he had "no substance other than my own soul in my body." Clearly, he allowed that essence to shine through in his portrayal of Gator. The glow of critical acclaim, including the special Cannes Film Festival award, made Samuel L. Jackson feel better than any drug ever could.

5

A HOLLYWOOD SENSATION

JACKSON EARNED MORE than critical acclaim for his appearance in *Jungle Fever*; he also earned more work—and bigger roles. His performance as Gator Purify had transformed him into the sought-after movie star he had always wanted to be.

Jackson had long dreamed of the day that Hollywood would come courting him. In the days before *Jungle Fever*, every call he made to his agent began with this question: "Did Hollywood call today?" The answer had always been "no." But when Jackson called his agent after the release of *Jungle Fever*, he heard a different answer. Hollywood *had* called. And Hollywood wanted *him*.

Jackson could hardly believe it. His dream had come true. Soon after *Jungle Fever* was released, he was flown to Hollywood, taken to lunch at Warner Bros. studios, invited to attend important meetings, and doing all of the other kinds of things he imagined big-name movie stars did. Before long, he was on his way to New Mexico to play misguided FBI agent Greg Meeker opposite Willem Dafoe in *White Sands* (1992). That same year, he also portrayed Mr. Simpson, the leader of a neighborhood youth club in *Jumpin at the Boneyard*. The film tells the story of a divorced and unemployed father who is reunited with his crack-addicted brother after three years. Neither *White Sands* nor *Jumpin at the Boneyard* were

Samuel L. Jackson, John Travolta, and Harvey Keitel in Quentin Tarantino's surprise hit Pulp Fiction. *Jackson nearly lost the chance to play Jules Winnfield—a part that Tarantino had written specifically for him—when he failed to take his first audition seriously. After he was granted another try, Jackson read so well that he inspired Tarantino to rework the ending of the film.*

box-office hits, but Jackson also appeared in the popular film *Patriot Games* (1992), based on the best-selling novel of the same name by Tom Clancy. Jackson played Lieutenant Commander Robby Jackson, a confidant and friend of Harrison Ford's character, ex-CIA agent Jack Ryan.

Just as he had done in his stage performances, Jackson worked hard to develop each film character he played. He now credits the diligence he learned in the theater for his ability to perfect his screen characters. "The fact that I am able to interpret material, to create a character, and create a whole character and not just a façade," he says, "is all due to the things I learned to do in the theater." Jackson took his research a step further, however. He began making up backgrounds and inventing entire biographies for his characters. In each movie, he wants to create not simply a character, but a *life* for each character. "I make up a lot of things about my characters so that I can have a whole person for myself," he said in a December 1998 interview with *Mr. Showbiz*. "I generally sit down and figure out when and where [the character] was born, what kind of educational background he had, what kinds of friends, hobbies—just little junk stuff for me that may not get mentioned [in the film]." An accomplished wordsmith, Jackson also seeks out roles that allow him to use his verbal abilities.

Why does Samuel L. Jackson go through all of this for his film roles? Because he wants moviegoers to be able to imagine that his character lived a real life before the events portrayed in the movie—and to be sure that they can envision a life for that character after the movie ends.

Jackson's technique has clearly brought him to the attention of movie critics, and it has also earned the respect of his peers. Charles Dutton, for whom Samuel understudied in *The Piano Lesson*, is amazed at the way the actor "becomes" the characters he plays. "Sam wants to make a physical character out of

Jackson took a break from portraying his signature "bad guy" characters when he appeared in the 1992 movie Patriot Games *as ex-CIA agent Jack Ryan's good friend, Lieutenant Commander Robby Jackson.*

each and everything he plays," Dutton remarked in 1998. "He does different hairstyles, puts on different vocal rhythms in his speech. . . . That's the kind of acting I enjoy." Jackson takes this kind of praise in stride. "I always have definite ideas [about] how I want the character to look," he told the *Toronto Star* in 1999. "I don't mind not looking like me. I'm not Tom Cruise."

Jackson's first starring role came in 1993 when he was tapped to perform in *National Lampoon's Loaded Weapon I*, a slapstick spoof of the popular *Lethal Weapon* action films that costar Mel Gibson and Danny Glover as undercover cops. It was the first time Samuel L. Jackson landed a role for which he didn't have to audition. His next film, *Amos and*

A menacing but hilarious Samuel L. Jackson threatens Mr. Potato Head in the 1993 comedy National Lampoon's Loaded Weapon I, *a take-off of the action film* Lethal Weapon. *The role was the first one in which Jackson starred—and the first one for which he wasn't required to audition.*

Andrew, was also a comedy. In this farce, Samuel's character is the wealthy and pompous Andrew Sterling, an anthropologist, playwright, novelist, and moviemaker who is mistaken for a criminal when he moves into an all-white community. "It's a story about how mistaken identity gets out of hand," Samuel said of the film shortly after its release. "And it deals with the sometimes ludicrous racial and class distinctions people often make."

Such distinctions occur not only on-screen but also in real life. And this kind of typecasting greatly disturbs Jackson. "The stereotypes they throw onscreen of [blacks] are generally the same. If it sells, then they want another. I mean, they want four Eddie Murphys. They want . . . five Martin Lawrences. . . . You very seldom see us portrayed as ordinary people doing extraordinary things or caught up in extraordinary circumstances."

Jackson continued his moviemaking career when

he appeared in *True Romance* and *Menace II Society* in 1993. He was also a hit as a chain-smoking systems manager named Ray Arnold in the box-office block-buster *Jurassic Park*. In the film, Arnold unsuccessfully tries to save the dinosaur theme park from becoming a disaster. In his attempt to restore electrical power to the park compound, he tangles with a herd of vicious velociraptors, and his severed arm is all that they leave behind.

While Samuel's star was rising in Hollywood, his wife, LaTanya, was busy with her own career, playing a character on the ABC daytime soap opera *One Life to Live*. Because of the nature of her job, LaTanya kept a steady, daily work schedule, while her husband's calendar was much more erratic.

Despite Jackson's previous successes working with director Spike Lee, *Jungle Fever* was his last appearance in a Lee production. A difference of opinion between actor and director arose when Spike Lee was casting for a new film, *Malcolm X*, which was released in 1992. It wasn't that Jackson disliked Lee or didn't respect his work. Rather, Jackson felt that Lee made promises, such as giving Jackson a role in his new movie, that the director never kept. Spike Lee knew he was going to cast Denzel Washington in the title role, yet he had Jackson read the part as a stand-in during auditions. And when Lee finally offered Jackson a role in the movie, he would only pay the respected actor "scale" wages—the minimum fee union rules required—rather than the higher salaries that more established and experienced actors usually earned. Only Denzel Washington would be earning more than scale in *Malcolm X*.

In Samuel L. Jackson's view, Spike Lee had become like many other producers in Hollywood—he was simply out to make money for himself. Lee claimed that his movie and the casting decisions he made weren't about money; they were about uplifting the black race. In a 1998 interview, Jackson recalled

Jackson as systems manager Ray Arnold and Richard Attenborough as the misguided billionaire who establishes a prehistoric amusement park in a scene from the Oscar-winning Jurassic Park.

his response to Lee's argument: "If this is about uplifting the race," he told the director, "then let me share some of the profits because you'll be uplifting the race by helping me."

Not long after the rift developed between Samuel L. Jackson and Spike Lee, Jackson almost blew his chance at landing the "big part" he had been working for. A few years earlier, Samuel had met independent filmmaker Quentin Tarantino when he auditioned for Tarantino's 1992 film *Reservoir Dogs*. The director/producer, who is known for his eccentric and almost obsessive ways, is also known as a Hollywood success story. Tarantino spent many years as a youth working in a video store, an opportunity that he used to study a broad variety of films and filmmaking techniques. After years of struggle, Tarantino's unique vision and groundbreaking style finally earned him a place in American filmmaking. *Reservoir Dogs* was his breakout film.

Jackson himself admits that he didn't do his best in that audition. Harvey Keitel, the actor with whom he was scheduled to read, didn't show up, so Jackson read opposite Tarantino and Larry Bender, Tarantino's producer. As a result, the actor felt thrown off his mark and didn't perform as well as he could have. Still, Tarantino was impressed, not only by Jackson's audition but also by his performance in *Jungle Fever*. While the screenplay for *Pulp Fiction* was still in progress, Tarantino contacted Jackson and told him that he was writing one of the characters with Jackson in mind. The role was that of Jules Winnfield, a smooth-talking, Bible-quoting hit man.

When a copy of the script for *Pulp Fiction* arrived, it came with a personal note from actor Danny DeVito, who was also one of the executive producers of the film. In the spirit of the film's plot, DeVito had written jokingly, "If you tell anybody about this, three guys from Jersey Films will show up and kill you." Samuel got the joke, but he also understood its true significance: this script was for his eyes only. The part of Jules Winnfield had been written expressly for Jackson.

When Jackson read the screenplay, he was awed. "I was blooownn away," he told *Premiere* magazine in 1995. "To know that somebody had written something like Jules for me. I was . . . overwhelmed . . . thankful . . . arrogant . . . this whole combination of things that you could be, knowing that somebody's going to give you an opportunity like that." Armed with the knowledge that the part had been crafted for him, Samuel didn't bother preparing when Tarantino's staff called and asked him to stop by the studio and read some of Jules's lines aloud. He figured he could do a "cold read" of the script without rehearsing it beforehand. But though Jackson thought he had done a reasonably good job, the producers were disappointed in his reading. They didn't think that he had instilled the character with the proper amount of enthusiasm. So they let another actor read for Jules—and they discovered that they liked that actor's reading better.

The producers called Samuel L. Jackson's agent and told him what had happened. Rather than give up his client's chance completely, the agent convinced Tarantino and the other producers to let Jackson audition again. This time, Jackson treated the opportunity as exactly what it was—a real audition.

Jackson was understandably nervous. He flew to Hollywood on a Saturday-night flight for an audition that had been hurriedly arranged for the next day. When he arrived at the studio, he grew even more uneasy. No one was there—no producers, no director; only a note addressed to him telling him they would be back momentarily. Matters only worsened when the producers and director finally did arrive. The real low point came when Tarantino began introducing Samuel to one of the producers, Lawrence Bender. Bender interrupted Tarantino, saying, "You don't have to introduce me to this man! I know him." Then he turned to Jackson and said, "I love your work. It's my pleasure to meet you, Mr. Fishburne."

The producer had confused him with another black actor, Laurence Fishburne. This producer didn't even know who Samuel L. Jackson was! Samuel was no longer nervous. Now he was angry. And he used that anger to fuel his audition. He read opposite another actor who was reading for the character that would be played by John Travolta. When the other actor started missing his lines, Samuel knew that he had nailed the character of Jules. The actor had become so caught up in Samuel's performance that he had become distracted from his own reading.

When the time came to read the final scene of the movie, Jackson was confident that he would do his best. After all, he had rehearsed the scene over and over. But at the last minute, as he was about to start reading before the producers, he decided to take a chance and read his lines differently from the way

he had rehearsed it. In his new interpretation of the scene, Samuel gave an entirely new dimension to Jules. When he finished saying his lines, the director and producers were dumbstruck. They were not only convinced that Sam was the right actor for the part but they also had a definite view of how the film would end. Samuel L. Jackson had clearly earned the role of Jules Winnfield.

Pulp Fiction is really three stories in one, but all of them revolve around underworld criminals of Los Angeles, California. The film cuts abruptly from one story to another. In the film's opening scene, for example, two petty crooks plan to hold up the diner where they are having breakfast, but just as they draw their guns, the film switches to another plot line, in which two hit men who work for a drug dealer are on their way to "take care" of some small-time dealers who failed to pay the "big man" his due. The third

Jackson's Pulp Fiction *costars John Travolta, Uma Thurman, and Bruce Willis (far right) joke with director Quentin Tarantino (center right) at the 1994 Cannes Film Festival in France. For his stunning performance as Jules Winnfield, Jackson received his first Academy Award nomination.*

Samuel with his mother, Elizabeth Jackson, in 1997. Samuel remains close to his mother and visits her in Chattanooga, Tennessee, whenever his schedule allows. In a 1995 interview, Mrs. Jackson admitted that she had wanted her son to become a pediatrician —but "that didn't go over too well," she said, because her son never gave up on acting.

story revolves around a boxer who is ordered by the same "big man" to lose an important fight so that the gangster can win a few gambling bets.

Of the two hit men in the film, Jules Winnfield and Vincent Vega (John Travolta), Jules is the more threatening. In contrast, Vega is soft-spoken, more concerned with recounting his recent trip to Europe than with terrifying his victims. (Vega's description of Big Macs and Quarter-Pounders at a McDonald's restaurant in France became one of the film's most memorable and often-imitated scenes.) Jules, by contrast, is larger than life. His bushy sideburns and mustache and his curly Afro hairstyle give him the appearance of having stepped out of another era. Tarantino explained that in the character of Jules, he wanted to suggest the kind of characters once featured in the "blaxploitation films" of the early 1970s. The term was coined by the industry publication *Variety* to describe the kind of movies in which blacks were primarily portrayed as promiscuous criminals or drug pushers, some of the very stereotypes that blacks were working to abolish.

Adding to Jules's character is the personality that Jackson himself brings to the role. One of the character's quirks is to quote Scripture just before he disposes of his victims. In a thundering voice that is at once that of a terrifying criminal and a fire-and-brimstone preacher, Jackson declares, "And I will strike down upon thee with great vengeance and furious anger those who attempt to poison and destroy my brother."

Of all the characters in *Pulp Fiction*, Jackson's undergoes the most significant and compelling change. After Jules is fired upon at close range and escapes without a scratch, he begins to question the reasons he has been spared, and he becomes convinced that he has been saved by God. When he quotes from the Bible again, he has dedicated himself to leading a different kind of life.

What is perhaps most remarkable about Jackson's portrayal is that, in spite of his character's violent and despicable acts, by the film's end the audience believes that Jules has truly turned his life around. Following his practice of creating a complete biography for his characters, Jackson imagined that Jules is the kind of person who faithfully attended church and Sunday school as a child. "He was a consummate professional," Jackson said of his character in 1995. "And [he was] a stickler for detail. He had this God complex. He was the person who controlled life and death in most situations. That's why John Travolta's character just stood back and let Jules do everything."

As for Jules Winnfield's fate after the conclusion of *Pulp Fiction*, Jackson imagines, "[he] starts traveling around the country, the world, getting into these adventures and meeting people. Now that doesn't necessarily mean that he stops killing people. . . . [W]hen he's out trying to find the true meaning of why he was saved, he still can fall back into the same things that he was into before. But not necessarily with the same kind of purpose."

Pulp Fiction's quirky plot, mesmerizing performances, and hypnotic but violent themes attracted moviegoers in huge numbers. Many film critics singled out Jackson's performance as one of the finest elements of the movie. The *Washington Post* called it "unforgettable"; the *New York Times* declared that his performance was inspired by "pure, fiery intelligence, making Jules the film's startlingly serious figure."

And then came the biggest news of Samuel L. Jackson's career: for his portrayal of Jules Winnfield, he was nominated for an Academy Award for Best Supporting Actor. Twelve-year-old Zoe, Jackson's daughter, called her grandmother in Chattanooga, Tennessee, to tell her the news. Samuel himself was delighted, but not surprised by the announcement. "I'm not shocked because everybody had been [saying it might happen]," the actor told John Shearer of the *Chattanooga Free Press* in February 1995. "But . . . I'm happy that I was finally able to get to the top of my profession."

In anticipation of receiving the award, Samuel practiced an acceptance speech over and over in front of a mirror. He wanted not only to accept the award graciously but also to send a special message to his mother, who had been injured in a car accident and was recovering in the hospital. Unfortunately, Samuel never got the chance to deliver his speech: the Oscar went instead to veteran actor Martin Landau for his performance in the movie *Ed Wood*.

Samuel L. Jackson was understandably—and visibly—disappointed that he had not been chosen. After the ceremony, he admitted that he was devastated. "I was disappointed!" he said. "Though in the days before the ceremony I had tried to guard myself against too much optimism. I began to think, Maybe . . . maybe. Just about everybody I ran into said they'd voted for me. . . . I made a bet with a friend that I would not be sitting there applauding and smiling like most losers."

Jackson may not have won an Oscar for his performance in *Pulp Fiction*, but he did earn an Independent Spirit Award, an honor bestowed on actors who are not affiliated with major movie studios. He also learned a very important lesson about the way Hollywood works. "Now, if somebody tells me they're writing something for me, I know I [have to] do the things I've always done to make sure that I get a job. I'm still being tested as an actor. Nothing can be taken for granted."

True to his word, Samuel L. Jackson would never take an acting opportunity for granted again.

6

BEYOND THE BAD GUY

HOLLYWOOD MAY HAVE finally come calling for Samuel L. Jackson, but the actor had no intention of becoming a stereotypical Hollywood movie star. In fact, he didn't even plan to move to the West Coast. Instead, he preferred to remain with his wife and child in their four-story brownstone in Harlem, New York. Though he lived in a troubled neighborhood where drug deals and violence were not unusual, Samuel felt at home there. "It's [a] black neighborhood," he explained in a *People* magazine interview some years earlier. "I'm used to it, and it's a comfort zone for me."

Unfortunately, Samuel and LaTanya's daughter, Zoe, was less at ease. Each morning, she traveled to New York's Upper East Side to attend school in a safer neighborhood. After she arrived home each afternoon, the sidewalks of her own neighborhood were off-limits because the threat of occasional gunfire made it too dangerous for her to play outside.

This was one of the main reasons why, in 1995, after LaTanya landed a role on a television show that would be filmed in California, the Jackson family left Harlem and settled in the homey Los Angeles suburb of Encino in California's San Fernando Valley. The job didn't work out for LaTanya, but Zoe adjusted very well to life on the West Coast, and her parents were reluctant to pull her out of school to return to

To Samuel L. Jackson, one of his most important roles is that of father to his daughter, Zoe, shown here in 1995. Having been raised without a father, Jackson believes in being a strong influence in his daughter's life. He admits, however, that his profession often keeps him from spending as much time with her as he'd like.

the East Coast. In addition, their new location allowed Samuel more convenience in pursuing his film career. It also allowed him to invest more time in his favorite new pastime—playing golf. The family decided to stay put.

After his triumph in *Pulp Fiction*, Samuel suddenly found himself being able to pick and choose among the roles he was offered. He could have chosen this period to take a break, to think over what he wanted to do next. Despite his growing fame, however, he believed it was vital to keep up the momentum created by his most recent success. And so he lined up a string of movie projects to keep himself busy.

In a 1994 interview, Samuel claimed that it was this choice that really furthered his career. "The closer together your jobs are, the greater producers think your ability is," he said. But LaTanya knew that there were also other reasons for his decision. Working hard was part of Samuel's personality—and it helped him stay clean. "It's his drug," LaTanya told the *New York Times* in 1997 of her husband's professional drive. "He had to replace [drug use] with something. As long as Sam has read a script or the camera is there, he feels as if he's been fed that day."

Samuel's relentless schedule might have kept him away from his family for long stretches of time were it not for the fact that in his next film, *Losing Isaiah*, he got his first chance to appear on-screen with LaTanya.

Losing Isaiah is the story of how a young, recovered crack addict (played by Halle Berry) attempts to regain custody of a child she abandoned in an alley three years earlier and whom she believed was dead. The child had been rescued by sanitation workers and brought to a nearby hospital, where a white, upper-class social worker (played by Jessica Lange) and her family decide to adopt him. What follows is a dramatic and emotional courtroom drama pitting Samuel L. Jackson, as the birth mother's attorney,

against LaTanya Jackson, as the white family's attorney. The other actors in the film were impressed with the Jacksons' professionalism on the set. "Their personal life never came to the job and that I really respected," said costar Halle Berry.

The movie gave Samuel a long-awaited opportunity to give his wife a few pointers about film acting. In a 1998 interview with Entertainment Television, Jackson claimed that LaTanya "was always criticizing how I did things, how I analyzed them, what I did, and she knew more about that process. All of a sudden when we got to *Losing Isaiah*, I had been doing films for awhile at that point . . . so all of a sudden I had the upper hand."

Samuel took only two days off after filming was completed on *Losing Isaiah* before he headed to the set of his new film, *Kiss of Death*. In this police thriller, Jackson plays opposite David Caruso and Nicholas Cage. Jackson plays a cop who sends

Jessica Lange, LaTanya Richardson, and David Straithairn in a scene from Losing Isaiah (1995), in which LaTanya and her husband, Samuel L. Jackson, played opposing attorneys in a child custody case. The movie marked the first time the Jacksons appeared on-screen together, and Jackson relished the chance to give his wife advice on film acting. "All of a sudden I had the upper hand," he joked in a 1998 interview.

Samuel L. Jackson in a scene from the action film Die Hard: With a Vengeance. *The actor's performance as Zeus was so good that the producer rewrote the script to give Jackson more screen time.*

another cop (Caruso) undercover to take down a drug lord (Cage). Cage and Jackson had worked together once before, in the film *Amos and Andrew.* But when they met again, Cage was struck by how much Jackson had matured as an actor. "He seemed like a totally different guy," Cage told *Entertainment Weekly* in 1995. "He looked different. He acted different. It was magnificent," Cage said of Sam's performance in *Kiss of Death.*

Just three days after finishing *Kiss of Death,* Jackson began filming yet another movie—*Die Hard: With a Vengeance.* With a back-to-back filming schedule, Samuel was spending most of his time away from home. He missed being in Encino with his wife and daughter. He especially regretted not having the time to do things a "regular" dad did, the kind of activities he took pride in doing during his time off, such as making beds, doing laundry, going grocery shopping, taking Zoe to school, and even cooking a lamb and pasta dish that was a family favorite. And, Jackson admits, his hectic schedule also affected his relationship with Zoe. "I'm sure that there have been many instances where Zoe has felt neglected by me," Samuel has said of this period. "Occasionally we have to fish around for ways to have a conversation about certain things."

Despite the regrets he felt over being away from his family, Samuel's involvement in *Die Hard: With a Vengeance* was a nonstop thrill for the rising star. The movie appealed to teen audiences about the same age as Zoe, and Samuel was a surprising hit as Zeus, a Harlem electrician who greatly distrusts whites. Zeus is forced to set aside his prejudices, and he becomes the sidekick of John McClane (played by Bruce Willis) when a mad bomber tries to destroy parts of New York City. Originally, Samuel's part was relatively minor. It mattered so little to the producer that when Willis suggested Samuel for the role, the producer said that he didn't care who played Zeus, "as long as Bruce Willis was in [the movie]." But Samuel played the role so well that the movie's triumphant ending was rewritten to include his character.

Jackson's role, as he viewed it, was to reflect the emotions of the audience watching the film. "In this film," he told *Newsweek* in June 1995, "it's my job to be an audience member, riding along with John McClane and reacting like a normal person would." His role was "not to be Superman but to approach everything like a regular guy on the street." The actor found Zeus easy to play, he said, because the character's personality was similar to his own. "I have the same attitudes toward education as this guy has, that I talk to my daughter about—she doesn't listen, but I talk—I have the same kind of acerbic wit he has. I tend to think that when pressed, I could be heroic in certain kinds of ways."

Die Hard:With a Vengeance was a modest hit, but though the movie itself received mixed reviews, critics unanimously praised Jackson's performance. Said the *New York Times*, "Jackson brings craftiness and pitch-perfect intensity to his role and . . . steals the movie from the ostensible hero and villain." Despite such acclaim, Jackson had to fight hard to land his next role, that of Mitch Henessey in the film *The Long Kiss Goodnight*. He had badly wanted the part ever since he'd read the screenplay, but the studio resisted—in part because the role had originally been written for a white man.

The incident just proved, Jackson said, that race still played a major role in Hollywood. Racial discrimination, he said in 1997, "gets attributed to a lot of different things. They can say, 'Yes, you're a great actor, but we need to get somebody with a little more box-office appeal who's done the leading man thing.' That's a nice excuse." Eventually Jackson appealed directly to the film's producer, Renny Harlin, to be considered for the part. The appeal worked. Jackson says he's "not interested in characters that are race specific. . . . Show me a good story with a good character and there's now [a possibility that] he could be black."

The Long Kiss Goodnight is a slightly unusual action film because it incorporates elements of romantic comedy. Teamed with actress Geena Davis, who plays Samantha Caine and whose husband produced the film, Jackson, as usual, had to find out where his character, Mitch, came from and what made him "tick."

In the film, private eye Mitch Henessey is Samantha Caine's only hope for survival. A small-town teacher with a seemingly blissful domestic life, Samantha actually has amnesia, which keeps her from remembering her real past as an undercover government assassin. As the film begins, both the government and the big-time criminals she failed to kill are out to get her. Jackson relished the job of dis-

covering exactly who Mitch Henessey is. In a 1996 interview, he explained:

> I felt that, on the inside this film, there was this great human interest story about these two people. . . . Samantha Caine's trying to find out who she is. And Mitch Henessey is this guy who has very low self-esteem and who's been truly damaged by a prison experience and his personal relationships. It was interesting to have him on the inside of this great big set-piece, making real discoveries about himself, finding some inner strength and some self-worth.

The Long Kiss Goodnight includes several spectacular action scenes that were difficult to shoot, especially in the record-breaking cold of Canada, where the filming took place. Jackson used a stunt "double" for a few of his action scenes, but he did most of them himself. "We did a lot of running and jumping and flying out of windows. We worked with an aerial crew—they taught us how to ride harnesses and still act at

In part because the role incorporated elements of romantic comedy, Jackson was nearly turned down for the part of Mitch Henessey, which he played opposite actress Geena Davis in the 1996 action film The Long Kiss Goodnight. *He had been told that the part was written for a white man, but Jackson believes that race is often irrelevant when it comes to playing well-crafted characters.*

As Carl Lee Hailey in the film A Time to Kill, Jackson played a black Southern man whose 10-year-old daughter is brutally assaulted by two white men. The role struck a chord with the actor, who not only had a young daughter of his own but also grew up amid racial discrimination in the South.

the same time," he later said. In spite of the grueling schedule and the frigid temperatures, Jackson had great fun filming *The Long Kiss Goodnight*. He also developed a lasting affection for Canadians, whom he found "laid-back, open, welcoming." His only complaint was that it was too cold on location to play golf. However, he did manage to attend a number of basketball games featuring his favorite team aside from the L.A. Lakers—the Toronto Raptors.

By 1996, when *The Long Kiss Goodnight* was released, Samuel L. Jackson felt ready to make deliberate choices in his career. He wanted meaty roles, substantial parts that he could get deeply involved in and that would allow him to use the techniques he had honed while an actor on the New York stage. He was anxious to become a box-office success, but he also understood the importance of accepting roles in movies made by independent studios. Such projects usually paid less and reached a smaller audience, but those audiences were usually more appreciative. Most of all, Jackson wanted new challenges. He didn't want to be someone who "coasted" on his fame. "A lot of people I found in Los Angeles came to Hollywood to become movie stars," he told the *Chattanooga Free Press* in 1996. "No one goes to Hollywood to be an actor." Jackson's aim, he said at the time, is to choose "tasteful" movies with good story lines and to take on roles that are "as diverse as possible." At the same time, he wants to present each of the characters he plays as unique and realistic.

As important as making tasteful choices is Jackson's conviction that each role he plays breaks new ground for blacks in the film industry. "There's more than one kind of black person," he told *Newsweek* in 1995. "Hopefully, somebody's realizing that there are black professionals who aren't carrying guns, and who speak intelligently, just like there are other characters I play—the black robbers, the black FBI agents, whatever. I can invest those people with real human values—as a black person. That will hopefully let somebody know it's really OK to have a friend like that. Because of lot of people don't know that."

Jackson's next two films couldn't have been more different from one another. In the comedy *The Great White Hype* (1996), he plays a flamboyant boxing promoter named Reverend Fred Sultan who decides to pit a white contender against his champion (played by Damon Wayans) in order to make more money. Jackson artfully combined the religious fervor of Jules Winnfield in *Pulp Fiction* with the greedy, do-anything-to-win mentality of some of his earlier bad-guy characters. That same year, Jackson portrayed Carl Lee Hailey, a black Southern man whose 10-year-old daughter is brutally raped by two white men, in the film *A Time to Kill*, based on the best-selling

Samuel enjoys his favorite pastime while raising money for Los Angeles police charities in May 1997.

novel of the same name by John Grisham. The movie centers around the murder trial of Hailey, a poverty-stricken factory worker who takes the law into his own hands to avenge his daughter's rape. Actor Matthew McConaughey, who at the time was billed as the next Tom Cruise, played the attorney defending Hailey's action. Sandra Bullock, Kevin Spacey, and Donald Sutherland also starred in the film.

The role took Samuel back to his own roots in the South. He understood from the start that he had a relatively small role and that his name wouldn't draw audiences. Nevertheless, Jackson delved deep into the heart and mind of his character, relying on his own background to give dimension to Carl Lee. "For the character, I walked pigeon-toed like one of my uncles, and I talked like one of my grandfather's brothers. I knew who my character was, and what he embodied." Samuel not only drew upon his personal history but also relied on his role as a father. "I have a daughter," he said at the time. "She's fourteen. I could understand what Carl Lee was going through."

While filming *A Time to Kill* on location in Mississippi, Jackson also discovered that the South he had grown up in had changed greatly—but not completely. He noticed interracial couples who seemed not to have any problems being seen together in public. "That shocked me," said Jackson, who was perhaps remembering the days when he had been punished for whistling at a white girl. But this more accepting attitude was not in evidence everywhere. The actor showed up at a Mississippi country club that had been recommended by the producer of *A Time to Kill*, who had also given Jackson a membership card. Jackson met with resistance. "The club members said, 'Wait a minute. Nobody said a Black man was going to be here,'" he remembers.

Although he was eventually permitted to play golf on the club's course, it wasn't long before he realized that he and his assistant suddenly had the entire course to themselves. Weeks passed before other club members would even approach Jackson. Even then, they were in no hurry to socialize with him. "One guy actually told me, 'Yeah I'd love to play with you. I ain't gotta like you to play.'" Another club member—who actually played a round with Jackson—claimed that had he done the same thing just a few years earlier, he might have been killed for associating with a black man. The racism Jackson experienced resonated on the evening news, where shocking reports about the torching of several black Southern churches aired during the time the cast was filming.

A well-deserved award: Jackson receives a hug from director Kasi Lemmons as the two accept the Independent Spirit Best First Feature Film Award for Eve's Bayou *in 1998. As a producer of the film, Jackson helped to get the project off the ground. "I'm still having a hard time dealing with the fact that someone can use my name and get a picture made," the actor joked after filming was completed.*

Despite such horrors, Samuel L. Jackson left Mississippi still feeling proud of his Southern background. Racial prejudice and discrimination still existed, but he chose to look at his homeland in a positive light. "The New South is very different," he said. "I'm very proud of the fact that I'm from there, and that it's changed in a whole lot of ways."

Jackson appeared in another film called *Trees Lounge* (1996), a well-done but critically unsuccessful film by first-time screenwriter and director Steve Buscemi, before Samuel returned to familiar ground—the South—for his next major film. In

Eve's Bayou, Jackson was not only a costar but also one of the film's producers. In fact, had it not been for Jackson's backing, the film might never have been made. Because it featured an all-black cast but was not the typical "'hood" film or comedy that earned big box-office dollars, Hollywood insiders considered the project a risky venture. Moreover, the film's writer and director, actress Kasi Lemmons, had only one big-time credit to her name, that of Jodie Foster's jogging partner in the 1991 thriller *The Silence of the Lambs*. But the name Samuel L. Jackson apparently had clout. After Lemmons convinced Jackson, whom she knew from their New York acting days, to join the project, the film seemed a little more solid to Hollywood. Having Jackson's name on the list of credits for *Eve's Bayou* meant that investors would be more willing to back the independent film. "I'm still having a hard time dealing with the fact that someone can use my name and get a picture made," Jackson marveled in 1997.

In addition to Jackson, the film also starred a number of other well-known actors, including Lynn Whitfield, who had won acclaim for her title role in the HBO movie *The Josephine Baker Story*; Debbi Morgan, known for her work on the soap opera *One Life to Live*; and Jurnee Smollett, a youngster who had appeared in the television shows *Hangin' with Mr. Cooper* and *On Our Own*, as well as in the film *Jack*. Diahann Carroll, a veteran stage, television, and film actress, also had a small role as a voodoo witch with a talent for spinning spells and casting curses.

When Lynn Whitfield heard that Samuel L. Jackson would play her husband in the film, the high regard she already held for him grew to new proportions. "It was very interesting to me that Sam decided to make this his first producing venture," she told Entertainment Television in 1998. "It actually happens to be pretty much a woman's story and a story about a group of people that we haven't seen very much in American cinema or world cinema. I really respect him for that." Whitfield pointed out that although Samuel could have chosen another vehicle—perhaps an action film in which he could show off his muscular strength—he chose instead to get involved in a simple, emotionally charged period piece.

Jackson's involvement went beyond his acting role and his financial support. He also polished the script and held auditions for every role. And after playing so many tough guys on the screen and working on sets where most workers were male, he also took on a new behind-the-scenes role: that of chief reconciler on the set. "I'm used to testosterone-driven sets," Jackson told the *New York Times* in November 1997. "All of a sudden, I was in an estrogen-fueled situation. . . . And I had to walk around and be the big-hug man," he confessed.

Eve's Bayou, which takes place in the early 1960s in Louisiana Creole country, begins with these haunting words, delivered by the film's central figure, a young girl named Eve Batiste: "The summer I killed my father, I was ten years old." Jackson is that father, a man named Louis Batiste, a popular small-town doctor who is a gentle parent and a seemingly good husband, but who is unable to turn down the attentions of the town's women. As usual, Jackson found parallels between Batiste, whose practice frequently takes him away from his family, and his own life as a film actor. His own family, particularly Zoe, suffered from his long absences, and he thought that *Eve's Bayou* might provide father and daughter with a way to talk about the situation: "Sometimes when we see things that look like us [in my films], then we can find a way to verbalize them by talking about what we saw. Possibly, that will happen with this film."

Batiste's need to feed his own ego is eventually his downfall. When Eve learns the truth about her father, she makes the only choice she feels is available to her, one that saves her family but sacrifices her father's life. *Eve's Bayou* offers a view of African-American life that is rarely seen on film: an African-American family of substance and means. "It's about a Creole family and it is dripping with the southern graciousness and glamour you've never seen in a movie about African Americans," Jackson's costar Lynn Whitfield said of the movie.

Eve's Bayou earned critical acclaim and was hailed by moviegoers of all races and backgrounds. It became the top-grossing independent film of 1997—and it was a film that would not have happened without Samuel L. Jackson.

7

THE FORCE IS WITH HIM

—— ❧ ——

BY THE TIME he completed *Eve's Bayou*, Jackson was ready for a new challenge—and he knew just what it would be. He had heard that director George Lucas was planning to film a "prequel" to his famous *Star Wars* series, and Jackson made no secret of the fact that he very much wanted a role in the new movie.

An avid *Star Wars* fan, Samuel L. Jackson had seen the first movie in the series on the very day that it opened in theaters in 1977. The movie mesmerized him. "It was everything I had always wanted a film about space to be—you know, guys with light sabers, really fast-moving planes, the costumes—everything was just right. It was like somebody had stepped into my mind and had taken everything that I wanted to happen and made it happen," he told *Star Wars Insider* magazine in 1998. The original movie also reminded Samuel of the pirate sagas he had watched as a child when he went to the movies with his mom in Chattanooga: "All of a sudden, here were guys sword-fighting again, with light sabers," he said. "I'm a huge Errol Flynn fan, and I watched all of *Commando Cody* and a bit of *Star Trek* and all those programs, but it wasn't the same for me. It was missing something, and George found all those things that were missing, and [filled them in]." The first *Star Wars* movie left Jackson feeling a kind of worshipful admiration for the movie's director and

The role of a lifetime: Samuel L. Jackson was overjoyed to win the part of Jedi elder Mace Windu in the eagerly anticipated prequel to the first three Star Wars films, Star Wars: Episode I—The Phantom Menace. *He also hosted a TV special in June 1999 that gave fans a behind-the-scenes look at the making of the blockbuster film.*

77

Veteran actor Dustin Hoffman and Samuel L. Jackson in the 1998 science-fiction thriller Sphere. *Although Jackson claimed to be nervous about starring opposite Hoffman, his apprehension was not apparent to movie fans.*

creator. As a result, when the opportunity arose to participate in the prequel, he was determined to find a way to do just that. In interviews and conversations, Jackson took every opportunity he could to talk about his desire to be in the next *Star Wars* film. He would do just about anything, he claimed, to get a part in the new movie.

His message finally got through to the right people while he was filming the movie *Sphere*, his first science-fiction thriller. Jackson played a member of a scientific team assigned to investigate a UFO that is discovered on the ocean floor. Although he had completed nearly 50 films by this time, Samuel was still in awe of his costar, Dustin Hoffman. He later admitted that he needed half a day just to get over his nervousness about doing a scene with Hoffman, whom he considers one of the finest actors in the business.

But what happened next was even more exciting. Jackson received a call from George Lucas's assistant inviting him to Lucas's Skywalker Ranch. Lucas had learned that Samuel was a *Star Wars* enthusiast, and he had also heard—as nearly everyone around Jackson had—about how much the actor coveted a role in his prequel. Lucas was considering casting Samuel L. Jackson for the new film.

Samuel could hardly believe his ears. "The call . . . was like the bomb," Samuel said. His response: "The real Skywalker Ranch? I'm leaving the house *right now!*" Not surprisingly, he loved his experience at Lucas's ranch. "Just an opportunity to go [there] was cool for me. I rolled on up there, and we sat down and talked, and had a great old time. George is cool."

As a result of that meeting, Samuel L. Jackson landed the role of his lifetime—the part of Mace Windu, which was written especially for him, in *Star Wars: Episode I—The Phantom Menace*, the first film of the *Star Wars* prequel trilogy. With the rest of the cast, Jackson headed off to England to begin shooting. Once there, however, he felt overwhelmed by what he was involved in. After all, there he was, in England, helping to create movie history with a man whom he considered one of the greatest directors of all time. He wanted to do his best. He didn't want to overplay his role, and yet he wanted to create a fresh, new character for the *Star Wars* saga.

Jackson grew even more nervous when he learned that he had only a very short time to prepare for the role. Lucas had demanded that the details of the movie, which was one of the most anticipated films in Hollywood history, remain secret, so even the actors weren't permitted to know the entire plot. Samuel did not receive his script until the day he first arrived on the set—and even then, he didn't have the complete script. Actors usually have several months, or at least several weeks, to prepare for their roles. Like other actors in *The Phantom Menace*, however, Jackson was expected to perform his scenes without knowing what was going to happen in the rest of the film. All he got was six pages—the six that featured his character—and his role was scheduled to be shot in only four days.

Jackson didn't have time to complete his customary preparations for the role. He wasn't able to create a biography for Mace Windu or to "invent" a background for the character the way he normally would have. For the first time in years, the actor was forced to rely simply on his instincts, to think on his feet rather than carefully prepare. To do this, Jackson based his portrayal of Mace on his own knowledge of the *Star Wars* tale—and relied on the confidence he had in his own acting skills.

Although he tried hard to relax and play the role naturally, it wasn't easy. "It's the kind of situation where you know you're keyed up in a certain kind of way because you're doing something that's interesting and exciting to you," he told *Star Wars Insider*. "I tried not to go in with any preconceived notion of what I was going to do and how I was going to do it. But I don't know if I achieved that. It's a strange sort of feeling for me, because I'm always pretty sure of what I'm doing."

Once George Lucas cried "Action," though, things started to flow for Jackson. He tried to infuse his character with as much realism as possible, especially because he was acting next to Yoda, the puppet character who first appeared in the second *Star Wars* movie, *The Empire Strikes Back*. Jackson also found working with other "alien" characters a singular experience. "I actually met actors I wouldn't know if they walked into my house today," he says, "because these guys were covered in make-up. There was one guy that I affectionately referred to as 'Calamari' [the Italian word for "squids"], because that's what he kind of looked like. And there was another guy . . . with a

duck on his head—I don't know what that was. You try to ignore that—that's the norm," he said of the weird costuming and make-up. "You just go ahead and do your thing."

Surprisingly, Samuel says that working with Yoda, a puppet operated by Frank Oz of *Sesame Street* fame, was not very different from working with a good actor. "He was there, totally involved, great facial expressions, great line reading, totally cool," Samuel said of the wise, big-eared character. The actor was fascinated by the way Oz turned a simple puppet into a believable character:

Director George Lucas (right) gives pointers to Alec Guinness, who is costumed as Obi-Wan Kenobi, during the filming of the first Star Wars movie in 1977. With all the secrecy surrounding the set of the 1999 Star Wars prequel, Jackson appreciated Lucas's relaxed approach to his job. "There was no tension, no pressure," Jackson said.

It's pretty special the way it happens. It's great because all of a sudden they'll say *action* and Frank gets in there and Yoda kind of sits up and does all this stuff, and then when George says *cut*, Frank takes his hand out and it kind of slumps over. But the guys that are operating his ears and eyes still have [them working], so his ears are still moving and his eyes are going, and he's kind of slumped over like he's . . . not feeling well or something. It's like, "Man, somebody help Yoda!"

When it came time for Jackson to utter the most famous phrase of the *Star Wars* films—"May the Force be with you"—he found himself breaking into a huge grin every time he said it. It wasn't that the line is funny; he was just so thrilled to be in the movie that he could barely utter it without smiling. But he forced himself to get serious. After all, this was *Star Wars*! "I had to wipe the smile off my face because it was important," he said later. "It is the crucial line."

When Sam's four days of shooting ended, he realized who the real master of the film was. It wasn't Yoda, Mace Windu, Anakin Skywalker, or even Darth Maul. It was the director himself. George Lucas "knows how he wants it to happen," Jackson told *Star Wars Insider*. "He hired us, he trusted us, so he's not giving us a lot of direction. . . . He's the first director I've ever known to have airplanes flying over [his head] and stuff falling around behind him and not yell *cut*. He'd just go, 'Yeah, that was good for me.'" Lucas's low-key attitude created a calm atmosphere that helped the film come together, says Jackson. "There was no tension, no pressure. People would have you believe that something that has that much secrecy around it would be a lot more tense or uptight, but it [was] not."

Even though he never did find out how the film would end or what would happen during the rest of the movie, Samuel L. Jackson returned to the States with high hopes. "I just hope this movie hits everybody the way it did the first time [in 1977]. It's the first part of a new trilogy and I hope I'll be around for the rest!"

Even if Jackson isn't available when the other films in the trilogy are shot, his action figure will be. The Mace Windu doll, complete with a blue-bladed light saber, was a best-selling toy even before the film was released. And whatever happens next in that "galaxy far, far away," Samuel got to say the classic film line—"May the Force be with you"—on-screen.

"How cool is that?" the actor said, reflecting on the experience.

Pretty cool for a regular guy like Samuel L. Jackson.

8

NEGOTIATING A FUTURE

❦

It would have been easy for Jackson to rest on his laurels after filming *Star Wars: Episode I—The Phantom Menace*. But he had work to do; he had other projects already under contract. He returned to filming with his usual energy, taking just a few days off here and there to work on his golf game.

His next film, *Jackie Brown*, based on the novel *Rum Punch* by Elmore Leonard, reunited Jackson with director Quentin Tarantino. In *Jackie Brown* Jackson plays Ordell Robbie, a small-time gun runner with a distinctive attitude and a braided goatee. Tarantino pursued Samuel for the role because of the actor's skill in interpreting his characters through their dialogue. "Sam gets the music out of my dialogue like no other actor does," Tarantino said in 1997. Samuel appreciated the opportunity to create that dialogue himself. "I . . . knew that Quentin was going to write [Ordell] some incredible dialogue. I'm a stage-trained actor so words are the most important thing to me," he explained. He also felt that portraying this character would be a particular challenge: Ordell certainly wasn't the first bad guy Jackson had played, but he had never played a character so "purely evil." Ordell, said Jackson, was the kind of guy "who'd kill you without thinking twice."

One of the highlights of the experience for Jackson was the chance to play opposite the renowned

Just a regular guy: Samuel L. Jackson in a tranquil moment in 1998.

85

Director Quentin Tarantino sought out Samuel L. Jackson once again for his 1997 movie Jackie Brown. *Sporting a braided goatee, Jackson (shown here with Robert De Niro) played yet another bad guy, Ordell Robbie, whom the actor described as so evil that he would "kill you without thinking twice."*

actor Robert De Niro. Jackson was amazed to find that De Niro seemed to be a very ordinary guy—a far cry from some of the dramatic characters De Niro is known for playing on-screen.

The film was well received by audiences and movie critics. Samuel's former buddy Spike Lee, however, took offense at the language used in the movie—especially the use of the derogatory term "nigger." Although the word is used in some of Lee's films, Lee believed the language was uncalled for and unnecessary to the meaning of *Jackie Brown.* He said that it was an insult to African Americans, and he accused Quentin Tarantino of being a racist. Samuel L. Jackson didn't agree with Spike Lee. The way he saw it, the language, while certainly offensive, is just the type that a character like Jackie Brown would use. "Personally," Jackson said bitingly in February 1998, "my feeling is that Spike's anger stems from the fact that he sat down and watched a good black movie and he hadn't made one himself in a while."

The adverse publicity over Lee's objections to *Jackie Brown* did not affect Jackson's career, however. Before long he began work on another blockbuster action film, *The Negotiator*. The movie is based on a true incident in which a hostage negotiator who is accused of murder and embezzlement takes hostages of his own in an attempt to prove his innocence.

Samuel landed the part of Danny Roman after Sylvester Stallone (of *Rocky* fame) passed on the role. Stallone had definite ideas of how he wanted to portray his character; he also wanted to make major changes to the script, including the addition of a female love interest. Jackson, on the other hand, didn't need all of that. He could identify with the character of Danny Roman just the way the part had been written. "[Danny Roman is] very much like me in that I know all the rules to most of the things I do," Jackson claimed. "And sometimes the rules do get in the way and you have to find a way to circumvent those rules to make things happen."

The deal was sealed when Samuel discovered that Kevin Spacey, one of his acting buddies from his New York stage days, was considering playing the other negotiator. Spacey's role is that of the expert who is brought in to talk Roman into releasing his hostages. Jackson had worked briefly with Spacey in *A Time to Kill*, and he relished the prospect of working with him again. Fresh from having won an Oscar for Best Supporting Actor in the *Usual Suspects* (1995), Spacey was looking for a new project. Together, the two actors decided to make the film.

As usual, Samuel did his "homework" on his character. He interviewed professional hostage negotiators and even spent some time with them on their jobs so that he could add realism to the film. In between bouts of hard work, Samuel also found time to fit in a golf game or two—but it was all in the name of research, he claims. "I played golf with a few of [the real-life negotiators]," he told the *Toronto Sun*. You spend four hours on a golf course with a bunch of guys, and you'll find out what they're about."

Despite the "golf research," filming *The Negotiator* was grueling work. Seventy all-night shots were run on the streets of Chicago, and 30 blocks of the city's downtown area were shut down during the shooting. Then there were the stunts. One scene, in which Jackson's character balances on the window ledge of a skyscraper, daring his enemies to shoot him, took two days to complete. Jackson did most of the work himself. "I was bolted to the floor on the 22nd floor, the windows were out, there were 'copters right in my face, and the wind was blowing," he said of the filming conditions. Jackson loves thrill rides and he usually doesn't have a problem with heights. But this particular stunt was almost too much for him. "I was shaking," he told *People* magazine in August 1998. "I would turn to the crew and say 'Okay, you're gonna catch me, right?'"

Jackson concerned himself not only with the twists and turns of such stunts but also with the convoluted plot. He added his own gestures and short passages of dialogue that made his character come alive. He even invented one of the many plot twists in the movie when he became frustrated in his attempts to figure out a way to make another character confess. Of this spur-of-the-moment gesture, he said, "It was just one of the many [innovations] that popped up that way."

Once filming for *The Negotiator* ended, Samuel headed back to Encino to resume the real-life roles of father and husband. Zoe was now 16, and she had begun dating boys. Jackson admits that he feels pro-

tective of his daughter, but he jokes that he doesn't need to fret too much about Zoe's boyfriends. "All the guys who come to date her are freaked out by me," he says. "They think I am Jules [from *Pulp Fiction*] so I don't have to lay down the law like most dads have to." In spite of his obvious ability to turn on the tough-guy behavior he's played countless times on-screen, Jackson considers himself a rational, down-to-earth person. He has always tried to impress upon his daughter that he is just a regular guy with a regular job. "I tell my daughter all the time that the only reason people think I'm special is that they watch me do my job. If they watched her teacher do her job then they might think she's special. If we traveled with the garbage men and watched them do their thing, then they would [seem] special."

Jackson was mesmerizing as a desperate hostage negotiator accused of wrongdoing in the 1998 film The Negotiator. *For his performance, he was nominated for a Blockbuster Entertainment award and an Image Award.*

Zoe's own ambitions may turn to acting some day, but at present she appears to have no such goals. When Jackson was asked recently whether he believed his daughter wanted to follow in his footsteps, he replied, "Not to my knowledge. She's in a theater class right now, but I really don't think so. She's a writer. . . . she's always been a critic." He explains that one day she decided to see *Pulp Fiction* with some friends. "I asked, 'How did you like it?' 'Ahh, it's OK, but that *Dumb and Dumber*, now that's a movie!'" Jackson relates.

Samuel L. Jackson is a regular guy to his fans, too. He is always willing to exchange character lines from his famous movie scenes or to give a fan an autograph. One youngster recently asked him what the middle initial *L* stood for in his name. "Lucky," the actor teasingly replied. And lucky is just how Samuel L. Jackson feels.

Even on the golf course, Samuel can't be bothered with the trappings of wealth and Hollywood success. He can afford memberships to expensive and exclusive country clubs, such as Los Angeles's Riviera or Bel Air, but instead he belongs to Mountain Gate, a golf community for serious golfers rather than golfing celebrities. And Samuel takes his golf game seriously —even if he does play a round or two with Sidney Poitier and Michael Jordan now and then. Perhaps this is because he sees many similarities between acting and golfing. In both activities, for instance, tension can interfere with one's performance.

Sam doesn't just golf to relax; he also frequently plays to raise funds for a specific cause or charity. He's a regular in the Bob Hope Chrysler Classic in Palm Springs, California, along with baseball player Roger Clemens; actor Joe Pesci; singers Alice Cooper, Michael Bolton, and Vince Gill; and former president Gerald Ford. Jackson also sponsors his own fund-raising tournament in Bermuda each year to benefit disadvantaged American youth.

A casually attired Samuel L. Jackson pauses to sign autographs during a 1998 appearance. "It's nice to know that people say 'I really enjoy your work' rather than 'I really like you,'" Jackson says. "It reminds me that I have a standard that I set that people recognize and respect."

Playing golf may be one of Samuel L. Jackson's passions, but if he could have chosen another career for himself, he says, it would have been professional basketball. One of his favorite players is Chamique Holdsclaw, who plays in Jackson's home state for the University of Tennessee (UT) Volunteers. When Jackson hosted the ESPY awards, a sports awards program sponsored by television's ESPN, he couldn't hide his admiration for her. He even wore basketball shoes that sported UT colors. He has also appeared in a Nike commercial where he is a different kind of fan—a fan of a group of teenagers who are playing "horse." When Jackson shouts, "Fan-tas-tic" at the end of the ad, he seems to mean it.

Samuel confesses to a few indulgences: his trademark hats, which are often the Australian brand Kangol, and his eyeglasses. (He owns more than 40 pairs and has paid more than $400 a pop for some of them.) And even though he's a regular guy, he still chases the elusive Academy Award for his work. In 1999 he won an award of a different kind—the Harvard University Hasty Pudding Award, which pokes fun at itself and at the actors and actresses it honors. The privilege has been shared by such stars as Sigourney Weaver, Kevin Kline, Katharine Hepburn, Paul Newman, and Harrison Ford.

Jackson shared his Hasty Pudding Award with actress Goldie Hawn. To actually claim the award, Samuel good-naturedly agreed to have his mouth washed out with soap, as "punishment" for the profanities he uttered in *Pulp Fiction* and other films. Then, he had to put on a brassiere and a wig and deliver his famous lines from *Pulp Fiction*—a quotation from the Bible—using a voice like Yoda's from *The Phantom Menace*. Only then was he given the small, gold pudding pot that celebrated his stardom.

For all its good humor, the Hasty Pudding Award is not the Oscar that Sam so badly wants—and feels he deserves. "In a fair world," he says confidently, "I guess I'd have three or four Academy Awards. *Jungle Fever, A Time to Kill, Jackie Brown, Pulp Fiction.* . . . But you know it's not a fair world. I'll just keep working."

And work he does. *The Red Violin*, an independent art film released in 1999, is the tale of a man who will do anything to own a valuable 300-year-old violin. Ironically, the part Samuel plays, that of a string instruments expert named Charles Moritz, was originally intended for his mentor and idol, Morgan Freeman. Freeman turned it down, but Jackson doesn't mind being the second choice in this case. "Following

Morgan is no problem," he says. "I thought their first choice was right on." In another movie, *The Deep Blue Sea*, released in the summer of 1999, Jackson starred with rapper LL Cool J in what he terms a "popcorn" movie, a science-fiction thriller about genetically enhanced sharks. Samuel described the movie as "*Jaws* Millennium" with "bigger, badder sharks than [*Jaws* director Steven] Spielberg ever dreamed of." His next character? Someone entirely different, a detective in the retro film *Shaft*.

A real movie buff himself, Samuel L. Jackson's desire is to continue portraying a wide variety of characters. "Now I want to do a slasher movie because I watched them. And I want to do a Hong Kong film because I watched them. I'd love to do a western. I could just imagine myself as a cowboy. And that's part of what this business is, being able to do things that you fantasize about as a child."

But playing characters who are worlds apart from one another is nothing new for this actor. Samuel L. Jackson has always been recognized for his ability to play diverse roles. "There's nothing you could dare me to do that I wouldn't try," Jackson told *Cosmopolitan* magazine in 1994. And as many moviegoers already know, there are probably few roles that Jackson wouldn't be able to take on successfully. Producer Lawrence Bender, who worked with Jackson on *Pulp Fiction*, claims, "He can do anything. I can see Sam doing [roles written by playwright] Tennessee Williams, stuff you don't normally see black people do."

Jackson is known for his willingness to adapt his physical appearance to the kind of character he is playing. Here, he plays a refined expert on musical instruments in the independent film The Red Violin *(1999).*

As a scientist in the 1999 movie The Deep Blue Sea, *Jackson confronts genetically enhanced sharks who develop near-human intelligence. About his widely varied choice of film roles Jackson says, "There's nothing you could dare me to do that I wouldn't try."*

Yet this kind of categorizing is one of the reasons why Jackson still has to fight to get the roles that he really wants. "It's a constant struggle," he told the *Toronto Sun* in November 1998. "People keep telling me I have a certain status in the industry yet they still balk when I want a certain role. Just recently, I wanted to play a priest in an upcoming film. The producers said they just didn't see him as African American. When did it matter what color a priest is?

They gave the role to Antonio Banderas who's Spanish. . . . It infuriates and puzzles me."

For Samuel L. Jackson, though, acting is more than just portraying the next character or acting in the next film. His work is all about self-discovery. "I like to do roles that allow me to discover hidden things about myself," Jackson has said. Whether that means coming to terms with his own drug addiction, as he did when he played Gator Purify in *Jungle Fever*, or acting out his own fantasies, as he did as Mace Windu in *Star Wars: Episode I—The Phantom Menace*, Jackson forms his own principles. "It's nice to know that people say 'I really enjoy your work' rather than 'I really like you,'" he says. "It keeps me from becoming a personality, and it reminds me that I have a standard that I set that people recognize and respect."

Recognition and respect are the two things that Samuel L. Jackson craves most. He has it as a golfer. He has it as a father and husband. And most famously, he has it as an actor. While he may never be Hollywood's traditional leading man, he will always be an actor of extraordinary integrity and dimension.

What is his ultimate mission? "To create a body of work that people can look back on and go, 'He was great in that!'"

Samuel L. Jackson has already done that. Mission accomplished.

CHRONOLOGY

———— ✿ ————

1948   Samuel L. Jackson is born in Washington, D.C.

1951   Samuel's father and mother separate; he is sent to Chattanooga, Tennessee, to live with his maternal grandparents

1958   Mother joins Samuel in Chattanooga

1968   Graduates from Riverside High School

1971   Is expelled from Morehouse College for participating in a campus demonstration

1972   Graduates from Morehouse after returning to college; forms the Just Us Theater troupe in Atlanta with LaTanya Richardson; lands a part in a Krystal Hamburger commercial and a role in the film *Together for Days*

1976   Moves to New York City with LaTanya; stars in *District Line*, *Home*, *Mother Courage*, and *The Mighty Gents* onstage

1980   Marries LaTanya Richardson; earns several minor film and television roles, including a part in the movie *Ragtime*

1981   Appears in the stage version of *A Soldier's Play*; meets Spike Lee

1982   Daughter Zoe is born

1987   Appears in *The Piano Lesson* at Yale Repertory Theater

1988   Appears in Spike Lee's movie *School Daze*

1989   Appears in Spike Lee's *Do the Right Thing*; severely injures knee in the door of a New York subway train

1990   Appears in *Mo' Better Blues*; successfully undergoes drug addiction treatment at a rehab center in upstate New York

1991   Stars in *Jungle Fever*; earns a New York Critics Circle Award and a Cannes Film Festival Jury Prize for his performance

1992   Appears in *Jumpin at the Boneyard*; *White Sands*; *Patriot Games*; and *Juice*

1993–94   Plays first comedic starring role in *National Lampoon's Loaded Weapon I*; appears in *Pulp Fiction* (1994); appears in *Jurassic Park*

1995   Moves with family from New York to Encino, California. Wins Independent Spirit Award and Best Supporting Actor Award from the British Academy of Film and Television Arts (BAFTA) for *Pulp Fiction* role, for which he is also nominated for an Academy Award, Golden Globe Award, and Screen Actors Guild

Award. Stars opposite LaTanya in *Losing Isaiah*; appears in *Die Hard: With a Vengeance* and *Kiss of Death*; is nominated for Golden Globe Award for TV performance in *Against the Wall*

1996 Stars in *The Great White Hype* and *The Long Kiss Goodnight*; appears in *A Time to Kill*

1997 Stars in *187* and *Jackie Brown*; stars in and produces the independent film *Eve's Bayou*; is nominated for Golden Globe Award and wins Blockbuster Entertainment Award and Image Award for his role in *A Time to Kill*; nominated for Image Award for *The Long Kiss Goodnight*

1998 Stars opposite Dustin Hoffman in the sci-fi thriller *Sphere*; costars with Kevin Spacey in *The Negotiator*. Is nominated for Golden Globe and MTV Movie Awards and wins Best Actor Award from the Berlin International Film Festival for performance in *Jackie Brown*; is nominated for Image Award and receives Golden Satellite Award for his acting role in *Eve's Bayou*; shares Independent Spirit Award for Best First Feature with director Kasi Lemmons and producer Caldecot Chubb for *Eve's Bayou*

1999 Named as Hasty Pudding (Harvard University) Man of the Year; is nominated for a Blockbuster Entertainment award and Image Award for for his role in *The Negotiator*. Appears as Mace Windu in *Star Wars: Episode I—The Phantom Menace*; stars in *The Red Violin* and *The Deep Blue Sea*. Produces *Caveman's Valentine* and *Mefisto in Onyx*; receives a star on the Walk of Fame at Hollywood's Mann's Chinese Theater

2000 Stars in *Shaft*, a remake of a 1971 film

FILMOGRAPHY

— ❦ —

Displaced Person (TV movie, 1976)
Ragtime (1981)
The Oprah Winfrey Show (TV appearance, 1986)
Spenser: For Hire (TV episodes, 1986 and 1987)
Eddie Murphy: Raw (comedy special, 1987)
Magic Sticks (1987)
Uncle Tom's Cabin (TV movie, 1987)
Coming to America (1988)
School Daze (1988)
Dead Man Out (TV movie, 1989)
Do the Right Thing (1989)
A Man Called Hawk (TV, 1989)
Sea of Love (1989)
Betsy's Wedding (1990)
Def by Temptation (1990)
The Exorcist III (1990)
GoodFellas (1990)
Mo' Better Blues (1990)
The Return of Superfly (1990)
A Shock to the System (1990)
Jumpin at the Boneyard (1991)
Jungle Fever (1991)
Law & Order (TV episode, 1991)
Strictly Business (1991)
Fathers and Sons (1992)
Ghostwriter (TV episode, 1992)
I'll Fly Away (TV episode, 1992)
Johnny Suede (1992)
Juice (1992)
Patriot Games (1992)
White Sands (1992)
Amos and Andrew (1993)
Jurassic Park (1993)
Menace II Society (1993)
National Lampoon's Loaded Weapon I (1993)
Simple Justice (TV movie, 1993)

True Romance (1993)
Against the Wall (TV movie, 1994)
Assault at West Point: The Court-Martial of Johnson Whittaker (TV movie, 1994)
Fresh (1994)
Hail Caesar (1994)
The New Age (1994)
Pulp Fiction (1994)
Die Hard: With a Vengeance (1995)
The Films of John Frankenheimer (1995)
Fluke (voice only, 1995)
Kiss of Death (1995)
Losing Isaiah (1995)
Mob Justice (TV movie, 1995)
The Great White Hype (1996)
The Long Kiss Goodnight (1996)
The Search for One-Eye Jimmy (1996)
Sydney (1996)
A Time to Kill (1996)
Trees Lounge (1996)
Eve's Bayou (actor/producer, 1997)
Jackie Brown (1997)
187 (1997)
AFI's 100 Years . . . 100 Movies (TV, 1998)
The Negotiator (1998)
Out of Sight (uncredited, 1998)
The Red Violin (1998)
Sphere (1998)
Caveman's Valentine (actor/producer, 1999)
Deep Blue Sea (1999)
Mefisto in Onyx (actor/producer, 1999)
Rules of Engagement (1999)
Star Wars: Episode I—The Phantom Menace (1999)
Shaft (2000)

BIBLIOGRAPHY

Chernoff, Scott. "Pulp Jedi: An Interview with *Episode I* Star Samuel L. Jackson." *Star Wars Insider*, 1998.

Cherrell, Gwen. *How Movies Are Made*. New York: Facts on File, 1989.

Dowd, Ned. *That's a Wrap: How Movies Are Made*. New York: Simon and Schuster, 1991.

Dreifus, Claudia. "Sam I Am." *Premiere*, June 1995.

Entertainment Television. *Samuel L. Jackson Celebrity Profile*. 60 min. Entertainment Television, 1998. Videocassette.

Hatcher, June Cooper. "Samuel L. Jackson." *Chattanooga Free Press*, 14 May 1995.

———. "That Busy Samuel L." *Chattanooga Free Press*, 27 October 1996.

Hobson, Louis B. "Samuel L. Jackson Gets Part on the Sly." *Calgary Sun*, 3 August 1998.

Jones, Maurice. *Spike Lee and the African American Filmmakers: A Choice of Colors*. Brookfield, Conn.: Millbrook, 1996.

Kirkland, Bruce. "Actor Plays Many Instruments." *Toronto Sun*, 13 November 1998.

Lee, Spike. *The Best Seat in the House*. New York: Crown, 1998.

Meyer, Nicholas. *Magic in the Dark: A Young Viewer's History of Movies*. New York: Facts on File, 1985.

Pearlman, Cindy. "Luscious Jackson." *Cinescape Insider* 4, no. 7 (1998).

Penfield III, Wilder. "Samuel L. Jackson Is Making Music." *Toronto Sun*, 17 November 1998.

Rochlin, Margy. "Tough Guy Finds His Warm and Fuzzy Side." *New York Times*, 2 November 1997.

Schoemer, Karen. "The 'L' is for Lucky." *Newsweek*, 5 June 1995.

Stoynoff, Natasha. "Bad As He Wants to Be." *Toronto Sun*, 26 July 1998.

INDEX

PICTURE CREDITS

TRACEY E. DILS was first published when she was nine years old. Today she is the author of more than 25 books for young readers, including *Annabelle's Awful Waffle*; *Whatever I Do, the Monster Does Too*; *Grandpa's Magic*; *Real Life Scary Places*; *Real Life Strange Encounters*; and *A Look Around Coral Reefs*. Her book, *A Young Author's Guide to Publishers*, received the Parent's Choice Award for 1997. Tracey is also the recipient of the prestigious Ohioana Award in Children's Literature for her contribution to the field.

When she isn't writing, Tracey spends her time in schools and community centers throughout the country as a "visiting author," conducting writing workshops and inspiring young writers. She lives in Columbus, Ohio, with her husband, Richard, and children, Emily and Phillip.

NATHAN IRVIN HUGGINS, one of America's leading scholars in the field of black studies, helped select the titles for the BLACK AMERICANS OF ACHIEVEMENT series, for which he also served as senior consulting editor. He was the W. E. B. DuBois Professor of History and Afro-American Studies at Harvard University and the director of the W. E. B. DuBois Institute for Afro-American Research at Harvard. He received his doctorate from Harvard in 1962 and returned there as professor in 1980 after teaching at Columbia University, the University of Massachusetts, Lake Forest College, and the California State University, Long Beach. He was the author of four books and dozens of articles, including *Black Odyssey: The Afro-American Ordeal in Slavery*, *The Harlem Renaissance*, and *Slave and Citizen: The Life of Frederick Douglass*, and was associated with the Children's Television Workshop, National Public Radio, the Boston Athenaeum, the Museum of Afro-American History, the Howard Thurman Educational Trust, and Upward Bound. Professor Huggins died in 1989, at the age of 62, in Cambridge, Massachusetts.